Irish Music Banjo Tutor.

The Tutor For Irish Traditional Banjoists And Other Musicians.

by
Owen Hackett

Publishers
Marieoin Publishers

*First Published 2001
by
Marieoin Publishers,
The Paddocks,
Ratoath,
Co. Meath, Ireland.*

© *Owen Hackett 2001*

*ISBN 0-9540554-0-3
Irish Music Banjo Tutor*

by Owen Hackett

*All the work in this tutor,
including Cover,
Concept, Design,
Drawings, Layout, Typesetting,
(Text & Music)
is the work of the author.*

**Printed by
Future Print,**
Grange Way,
**Baldoyle Industrial Estate,
Dublin 13,
Ireland**

*All rights reserved. No part of this publication may be reproduced, stored in a retrieval system or transmitted, in any form or by any means, electronic, mechanical, photocopying, visual, recordings, or by any other means whatsoever, without the prior written permission of the publisher or his agents.
This tutor is sold subject to the condition that it shall not, by way of trade or otherwise, be lent, re-sold, or otherwise circulated without the publisher's written consent in any form of binding or cover, other than that in which it is first published.
Copying is stealing from the author.
This tutor is protected by copyright law.*

ACKNOWLEDGMENTS

*To My Parents,
Tommy & Molly Hackett (RIP)
from whom I inherited the love of the Irish Music,
and who showed great patience and love
as I learned the instrument.*

1 Co 12: 4 - 7

*There are many different gifts,
but it is always the same Spirit;
there are many different ways of serving,
but it is always the same Lord.
There are many different forms of activity,
but in everybody it is the same God who is at work in them all.
The particular manifestation of the Spirit granted to each one
is to be used for the general good.*

*Lord, without Your Holy Spirit
I would be unable even to lift my little finger.*

Thank You.
Owen Hackett

IV

FOREWORD

This tutor by Eoin Hackett will be welcomed by teachers and students of the banjo alike. It presents a great variety of tunes - airs, marches, polkas, jigs and reels - all specially chosen and styled for the banjo. It gives detailed help and advice on the best techniques to use with each tune, and follows a progressive path from an introduction to the banjo right up to the playing stage, all the time building on what has been learned as well as presenting a new challenge for the learner.

Eoin has been playing the banjo for over 30 years. In that time he has played widely and built up a large repertoire of Irish music. He also has a number of fine compositions to his credit, and some of these are included here. He has a nice easy traditional style, soft and sympathetic to the music.

This tutor will be of great assistance to young and old alike who are students of the banjo. It will give them first hand help from one of Irelands finest banjo players.

ANTOIN MAC GABHANN

*My
grateful thanks to
Marie and our five children for
putting up with and encouraging me
as I created and worked on this tutor.
I would also like to thank my parents, who
passed on to me their love of music and taught me
my first tunes.*

Why the banjo?
*Sometime in the late 1950's I had tried to play the tin whistle,
but I couldn't control the temperamental nature of the
instrument, I never thought of blaming myself. Anyway, one day
around 1960-63; I had to cycle from Tullamore to Cappincur,
(three & half miles) to my Grandparent's house, to get a bag of
potatoes for my Mother. My Grandmother showed me a banjo which
my uncle Frank had left behind (after one of his visits home from
England) with instructions that she could sell it if she wanted to. She
must have seen my face light up as I plucked the strings, for a week
later, after telling my Mother about this marvellous banjo, my
Mother arrived back from my Grandparents house with the banjo
hanging on the handlebars of her bike. My Mother had given her a
coat for one of my aunts and ten shillings (half an Irish Pound) for
herself for the banjo. My friends whom I played with every day,
instantly lost a goalkeeper.
Nobody I knew at that time, had any idea how the banjo
should be tuned, so after a long time trying to play it
incorrectly tuned, (on one occasion tuned like a base
guitar), I managed to buy a tutor for a mandolin which
I improvised to suit my needs.
I would also like to thank Tony Smith
(Antoin Mac Gabhann) who Proof read the
tutor, and Michael O' Reilly who
named the notes for me, on the
Concertina.*

*Note: Owen has been teaching the Banjo since the mid 1970's.
He also won Four Senior All Ireland Medals Playing the Banjo.
Three Solo Playing and One with a Ceili Trio,
with Ellen Flanagan (Accordian)
& Eugene Nolan (Flute).*

Table of Contents

About The Banjo

	Page
Buying A Banjo	1
Using The Strap	2
Positioning The Bridge	3
The Plectrum And How To Hold It	4
Using The Fretboard	5
Strings And Different Banjos	6
Fitting New Strings	7
Vellum The	84-86

Key Charts For Some Commonly Used Instruments

	Page
Concert Flute & Whistle Key Chart	8
Accordion Key Chart	9
Concertina Key Chart	10
Banjo, Mandolin, Violin, Bouzouki, & Other Key Charts	11
Important Stuff	12
Scales	13
Basic Exercises	14

Your First Tunes

Tune	Page	Lesson No.	Type	Time Sig,	Key
Twinkle Twinkle Little Star	15	1	Miscellaneous	2/4	A
Baa Baa Black Sheep	19	2	Miscellaneous	2/4	D
Jingle Bells	21	3	Polka	2/4	G
Row Row Your Boat	24	4	Miscellaneous	2/4	D
London Bridge	24	4	Miscellaneous..	2/4	C
Baidin Fheilimi	25	5	Waltz	3/4	C
Spancil Hill	29	6	Waltz	3/4	Bm
Shoe The Donkey	31	7	Mazurka	3/4	G
An Fhalaingin Mhuimhneach	32	8	Mazurka	3/4	G
Idle Road	33	9	Double Jig	6/8	G
Bryan O'Lynn	35	10	Double Jig	6/8	Am
Biddy's Wedding	36	11	Double Jig	6/8	C
Paddy's Return	37	12	Double Jig	6/8	D
Absent Minded Man	38	13	Double Jig	6/8	A
O'Gallagher's Frolics	40	14	Double Jig	6/8	Dm
Drops Of Brandy	41	15	Slip/Hop Jig	9/8	G
I Have A Wife Of My Own	43	16	Slip/Hop Jig	9/8	G
Hunting The Hare	45	17	Slip/Hop Jig	9/8	D
Dever The Dancer	46	18	Slip/Hop Jig	9/8	Bm
Barney Bralligan	47	19	Slip/Hop Jig	9/8	D
Boy's Of Bluehill	49	20	Hornpipe	4/4?	D
Harvest Home	51	21	Hornpipe	4/4?	D
Friendly Visit	53	22	Hornpipe	4/4?	G
Swan The	56	23	Hornpipe	4/4?	G
Kerry Polka	58	24	Polka	2/4	D
Maria's Polka	59	25	Polka	2/4	G
Polka	61	26	Polka	2/4	A
Cadum Woods Polka	62	27	Polka	2/4	G
Slide	64	28	Slide	12/8	D
Dingle Regatta	65	29	Slide	12/8	G
Going To The Well For Water	66	30	Slide	12/8	D
Trip To Durrow	67	31	Reel	4/4 or (C)	D
Bunch Of Keys	69	32	Reel	4/4 or (C)	G
Dawn The	71	33	Reel	4/4 or (C)	G
Come West Along The Road	72	34	Reel	4/4 or (C)	G
Teresa's Smile	73	35	Reel	4/4 or (C)	G
Innocent Child The	74	36	Reel	4/4 or (C)	C
Retreat the	75	37	Reel	4/4 or (C)	Dm
John Brady's March	76	38	March	2/4	G
Playing in Different Keys	78	Advanced			
Transposing	81	Advanced			
Some Tunes to Play.	87				

VIII Index

Below, you will find references to pages where many of the terms and names used throughout the tutor can be found. Note that all the pages where these can be found are not listed here. Only some key pages or early mention of a particular term is listed. An example of this would be '1st. ending sign'. It is only listed here a few times, but can be found on many pages.

Term	Pages		Term	Pages
1st ending sign	21, 23, 24 31 etc.		Minor	29, 35...
2/4 time	15, 19, 21,24,58,59, 61, 62		Natural	12...
2nd ending sign	21, 23,		Note values (length)	17, 12...
3/4 time	25, 29, 31, 32...		Nut	3, 11.
6/8 time	33, 35, 36, 37, 39, 40...		Octave	78.
9/8 time	41, 43, 45, 46, 47...		Ornamentation	38.
12/8 time	64, 65, 66...		Pitch	7, 12.
Accents	15...		Playing in different keys	78, 79.
Accidentals	74...		Plectrum	5, 13, 14, 17...
Accordion key-chart	9...		Polka	20, 21...
Action	6...		Quadruplet	48...
Active	1...		Quaver	12, 7, 21, 26, 27,
Arm-rest or Rim	5...		Reciprocal strokes	34.
Banjo keyboard	11...		Repeat sign	20, 21, 22, 24, 31,34...
Bar lines	15...		Resonator	6.
Barring/Stopping notes	57,69...		Rest	12...
Beat	15, 17, 18, 20...		Rhythm	23, 24...
Begin repeat	21, 23, 37...		Scales	13...
Beginning	15...		Semibreve	12...
Bent	1...		Semiquaver	12...
Bridge (position of)	3, 6...		Semitone	20, 12, 14, 15...
Buzzing- Burring	1...		Sharp (sharpened)	12, 14, 15, 20...
Capo'	79...		Size	1,
Common or 4/4 time	49, 51, 53, 56,67, 69...		Slur	55, 71
Concertina key-chart	10.		Staff- Staves	12...
Count (ing)	15, 18, 17...		Steady	15...
Crotchet	12, 13, 17, 18, 20, 21, 26..		Strap	1,
Demisemiquaver	12...		Strings	1, 7, 8,
Dotted crotchet	52, 45...		Strokes (Plectrum)	17...
Dotted minim	23, 25 29...		Thumb	6...
Emphasis	20, 33...		Tic, Tied notes	29...
End repeat	37...		Time signatures	73...
End sign	34...		Timing	13...
Equal	15...		Tone	6, 7...
Fingerboard	1, 27...		transpose	74, 81...
Fingers - position	6, 15, 30...		Treble	20, 36...
Flagged note	39...		Treble (clef) sign	12, 13, 73...
Flat	12...		Tremolo	21...
Fluctuating	60...		Trill	36...
Frets-Fretboard	1, 6, 17...		Triplet(s)	21, 24, 36...
Grace note	70...		Tuning	7, 8, 15...
Key signature	14, 18...		Twist	1.
Leger lines	25...		Vellum	3, 5,83...
Machine heads	8...		Waltz time	25...
Major	13, 16...		Warp	1.
Melody	24...		Whole note	12...
Minim	12, 17, 18, 26, 27...			

BUYING A BANJO

If buying for a child, the first thing to remember is the <u>size.</u> How often one sees a small child peering over the top of too large an instrument.

The child will eventually grow big enough to be able to handle a large instrument, but by then the effort of trying to play it could result in the child giving it up altogether.

Badly worn frets can cause 'buzzing' and cause the banjo to play out of tune. The worn frets allow the strings to drop *below* the level of the active fret, thus allowing the string to slightly touch the next fret while it is vibrating. This causes a buzzing sound. *see diagram below.*

Check banjo for twist, by holding it up to eye level and looking along the length of the fingerboard.
Do this from both ends.

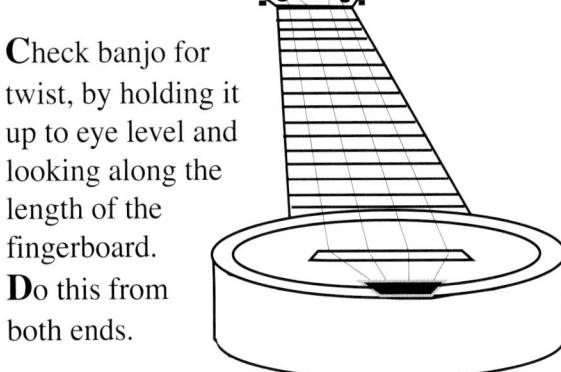

Check the frets up along the fretboard by playing a tune and listening that there are still in tune, and the frets are not buzzing at this higher level. Sometimes, on inexpensive instruments, higher level frets may be fitted carelessly as they are not as much in demand.

Another thing to watch for is an excessively bent fretboard.

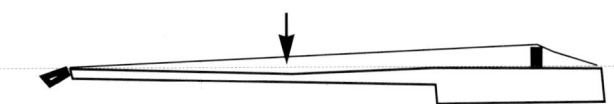

Section of fingerboard showing twist or warp.

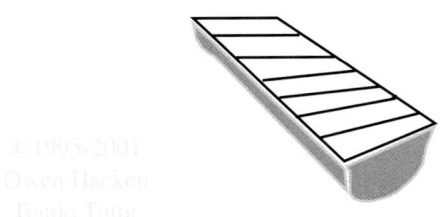

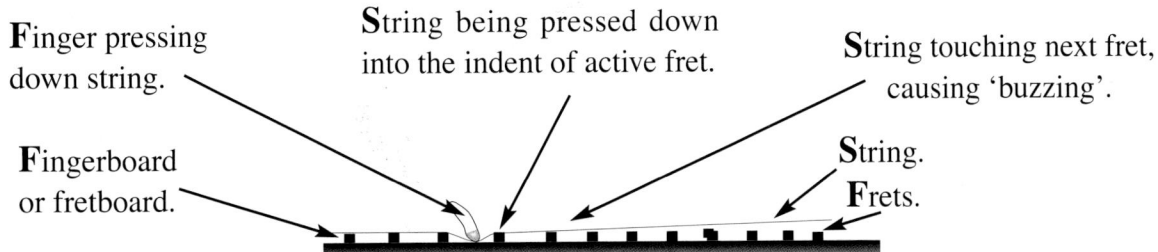

Finger pressing down string.

String being pressed down into the indent of active fret.

String touching next fret, causing 'buzzing'.

Fingerboard or fretboard.

String.
Frets.

USING A STRAP

The use of a strap is recommended. It holds the instrument securely in position, and allows the player to concentrate solely on playing the instrument. But please note that the design of the strap, and *where* it is fitted on the banjo is important

A wide strap or one with a soft adjustable shoulder pad, is suggested. *A narrow one cuts into young shoulders and causes discomfort.*

This banjo player likes to use a strap to hold the banjo, but he overlooked adjusting it's length to suit himself.
The height of the banjo will change when he sits down

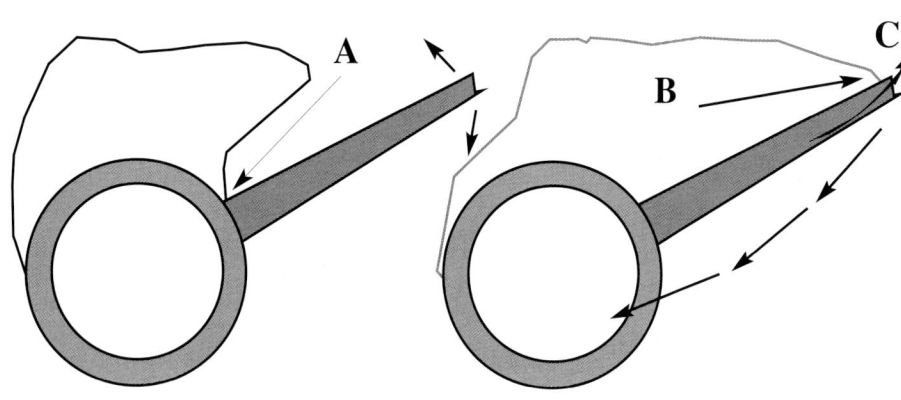

position A. is to be preferred as it allows the neck of the banjo to be freely rotated.

In position B, the banjo will swing in the direction of the arrows if released even for a moment. More important; the fret-board can be pulled out of line, causing warps & twists. (Arrow 'C')

The strap should be adjusted so that the banjo is just resting on your lap when you sit down to play.

Distance A *see diagram* should equal distance B. This means that the playing position will always be the same whether you sit or stand.

POSITIONING THE BRIDGE

3

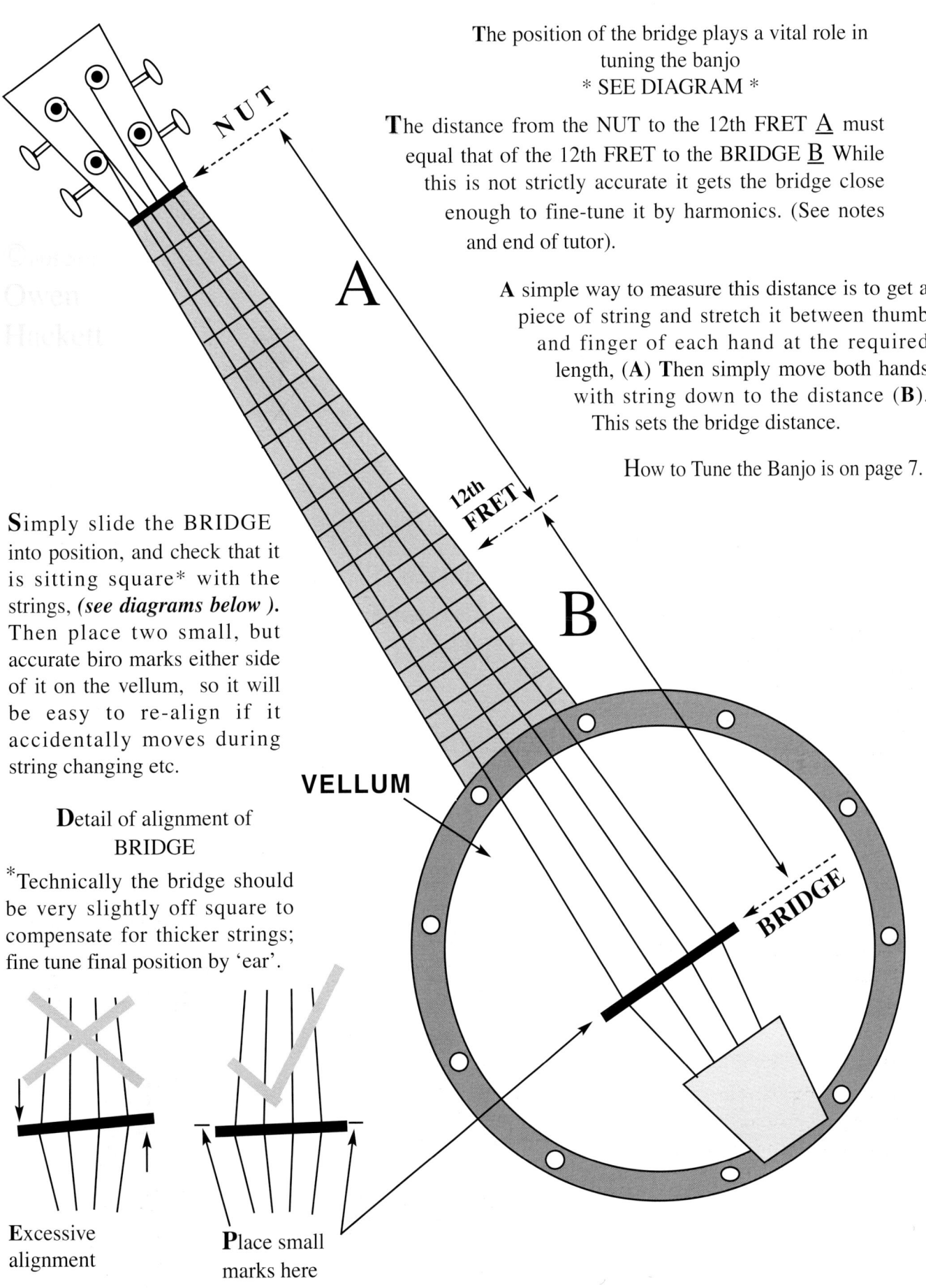

The position of the bridge plays a vital role in tuning the banjo
* SEE DIAGRAM *

The distance from the NUT to the 12th FRET <u>A</u> must equal that of the 12th FRET to the BRIDGE <u>B</u> While this is not strictly accurate it gets the bridge close enough to fine-tune it by harmonics. (See notes and end of tutor).

A simple way to measure this distance is to get a piece of string and stretch it between thumb and finger of each hand at the required length, (**A**) Then simply move both hands with string down to the distance (**B**). This sets the bridge distance.

How to Tune the Banjo is on page 7.

Simply slide the BRIDGE into position, and check that it is sitting square* with the strings, *(see diagrams below)*. Then place two small, but accurate biro marks either side of it on the vellum, so it will be easy to re-align if it accidentally moves during string changing etc.

Detail of alignment of BRIDGE

*Technically the bridge should be very slightly off square to compensate for thicker strings; fine tune final position by 'ear'.

Excessive alignment

Place small marks here

4 THE PLECTRUM AND HOW TO HOLD IT

Choosing the right plectrum is very important. The plectrum should be firm yet flexible (springy) near the point so as to be able to *FLICK* the string quickly and still be instantly ready to sound the next note.

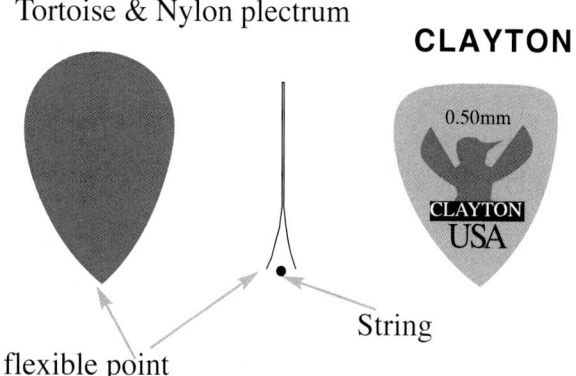

Tortoise & Nylon plectrum
CLAYTON 0.50mm
flexible point
String

Holding the plectrum properly enables you to play better.

Hold the plec' firmly, but not too tightly between thumb and 1st finger, and play down ↓ (towards the ground), then up ↑ again (towards your face).

Sometimes players use a plec' that is too light, and twist it between thumb and finger to stiffen it up, but this impairs their playing & tone. **A**lways use proper strength plectrums.

There are many types of plecs on the market, not all suitable for banjo playing. **T**hick inflexible plectrums give a dull, unmusical thud, instead of a bell-like ring which can be produced by proper use of a good plec' striking good strings.
CLAYTON USA
(made from Acetate) is very good, being close to *(tortoise shell which cannot be readily found.)* and is graded with a thickness/strength number, Stick to the grade that you find best. **T**he triangular plectrum shown above is good also, having three playing points each a different thickness and numbered to reflect this. **B**eginners might like to try point no.1 until they have mastered a steady rhythm of up and down movements.

Important! keep your wrist and hand relaxed; if you tend to tense up, look at your hand and tell it to relax by directing your thoughts towards it.

Resting you arm on the banjo rim or arm-rest, bend your wrist over the bridge and strings, <u>without</u> touching them; as shown in the diagram.

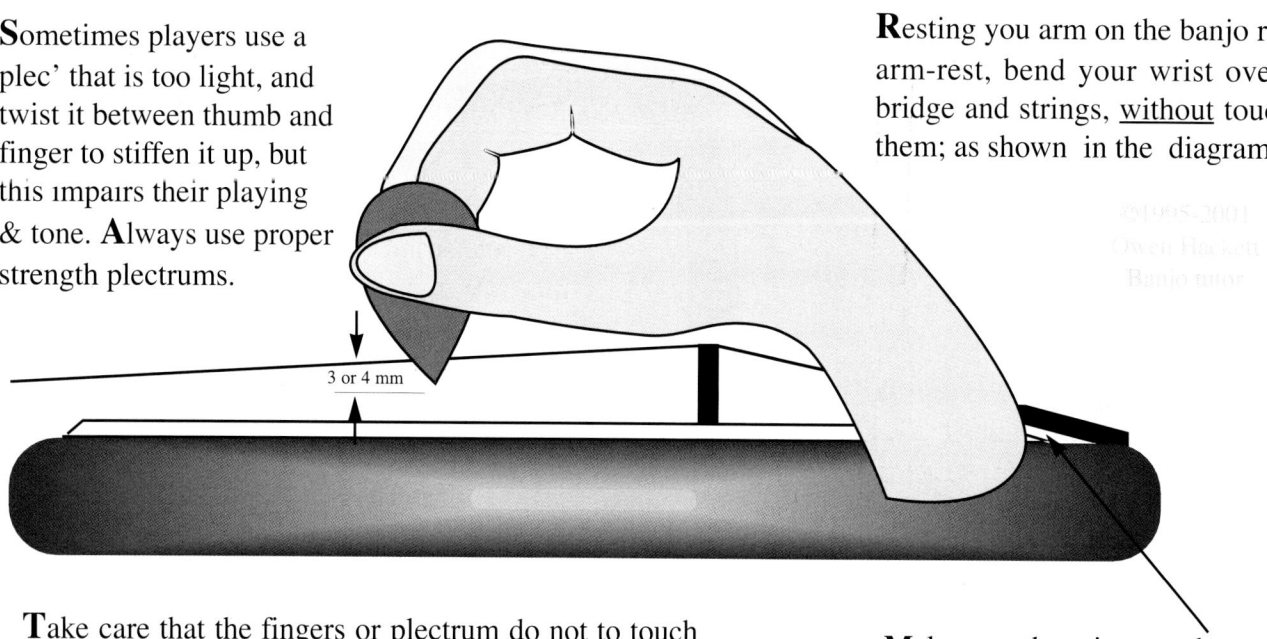

3 or 4 mm

Take care that the fingers or plectrum do not to touch the vellum . The plec' should protrude no more than only about 3 or 4 mm below the strings.

Make sure there is a gap here.

USING THE FRET-BOARD

The fingers on the fretboard hand should point back towards the shoulder, or back along the fingerboard as much as possible in the direction of the arrows. This position makes it much easier to reach the high notes quickly.

Note position of fingers.
(2 frets per finger).

Keep thumb lightly pressed against fingerboard, and use it as a swivel point. You should, with a little practice, be able to reach right up the fingerboard without moving thumb.

<u>Do not allow</u> thumb to come around over the top of fingerboard. This will limit your reach.

← 1st finger
← 2nd finger
← 3rd finger
← 4th finger

A good choice of bridge is essential for good tone. An unsuitable bridge will not transmit the string vibrations properly, resulting in poor quality sound. Try different types until you're satisfied with the sound. If a bridge is too high, the 'action' of the strings might also be too high (see **A** below) and the fingers will most likely get sore from pressing the strings down the extra distance to the frets. The strings may also be stretched out of tune.

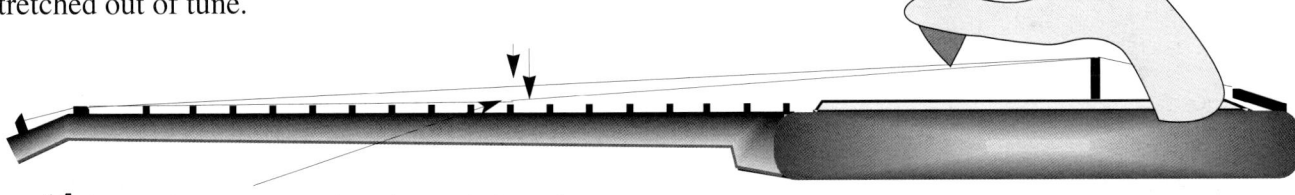

(**A**) Extra distance causes string to be stretched out of tune

Another cause of strings being stretched out of tune is the angle of the (neck) fretboard being mis-aligned. Removing the resonator (back) will reveal whether you can make mechanical adjustments by means of screws for this purpose. Be careful; tampering here is not recommended unless you are sure of what you are doing. Leaving it to the experts is advised.

To get the best tone from your banjo, strike the strings about 1-1/4 - 2 inches (30 - 50 mm) from the bridge. This position varies slightly from banjo to banjo due to different length instruments. Experiment for yourself.

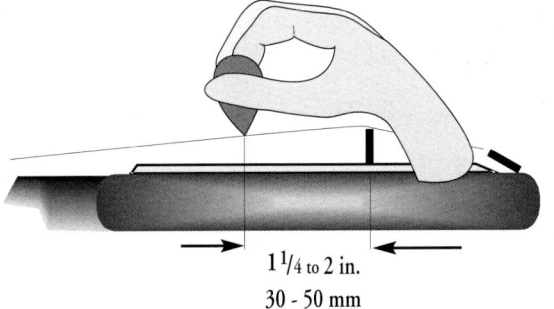

1 1/4 to 2 in.
30 - 50 mm

STRINGS AND DIFFERENT LENGTH BANJOS

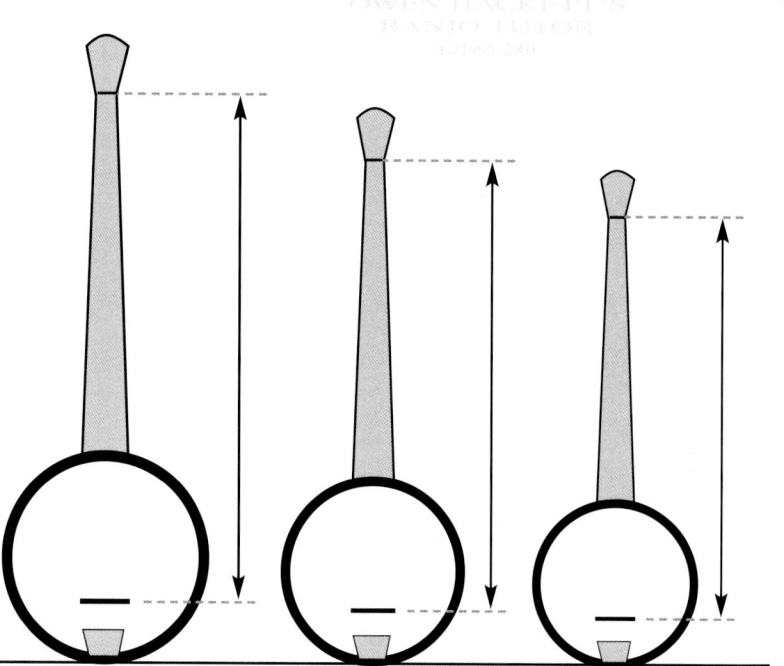

Unlike the standard full size violin, banjos come in different sizes. This can be a problem when tensioning strings to the required pitch.

With standard tenor banjo strings, tuning to one octave below concert pitch (*Irish tuning like the violin*) can result in loose strings; which sound awful. On the longer Plectrum banjo (*a close relation to the 'G' banjo*) the strings tension up fine because of the extra length.

Thickness of strings are measured in standard wire gauge; inches or millimetres. For example, the following list is taken from a standard set of tenor banjo strings. These may vary slightly from manufacturer to manufacturer.

String No.	1st	2nd	3rd	4th
Thickness	.0009in 0.229mm	.016in 0.406mm	.023in 0.584mm	.030in 0.762mm
Tenor tuning	A	D	G	C
Concert tuning	E	A	D	G

Tip
To maintain a good quality sound, change the full set of strings after every 15-20 hours playing. String which are kept stretched eventually lose their ring and give off a dull sound.

The problem of tuning tenor strings <u>A-D-G-C. up</u> to the required <u>E-A-D-G</u> is obvious; the thinner strings snap long before they get to the required pitch. They have to be tuned <u>down</u> to the <u>E-A-D-G</u> an octave lower. The problem here is that the strings are now not tight enough (they have not reached their proper tension) so do not give a clear, sharp tone. The answer many banjo players have come up with, is to try guitar strings; the most popular being 1st, 2nd, 4th, & 5th.

Tom Cussens, manufacturer of quality hand made banjos has solved the problem. He has strings specially designed to his own specifications, made in Germany.

See his display advertisement in this tutor

FITTING NEW STRINGS.

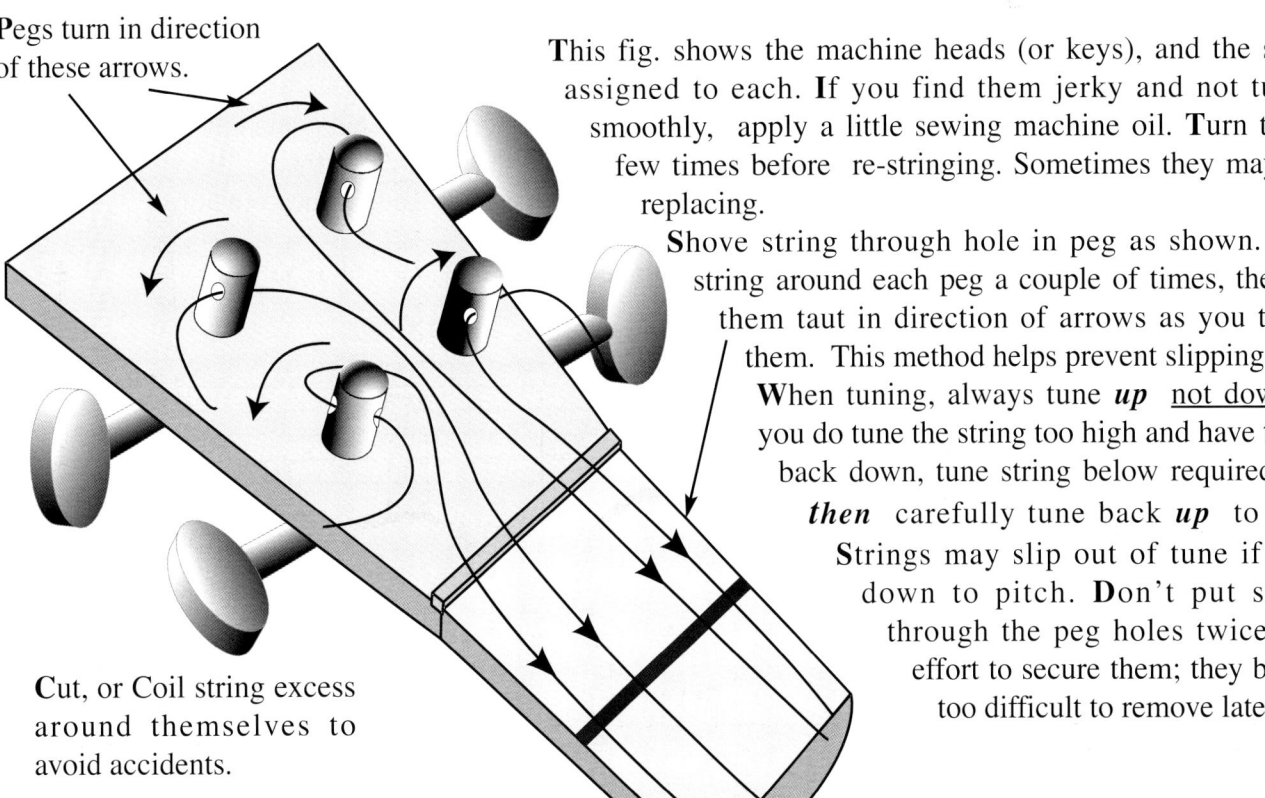

Pegs turn in direction of these arrows.

Cut, or Coil string excess around themselves to avoid accidents.

This fig. shows the machine heads (or keys), and the strings assigned to each. **I**f you find them jerky and not turning smoothly, apply a little sewing machine oil. **T**urn them a few times before re-stringing. Sometimes they may need replacing.

Shove string through hole in peg as shown. **W**ind string around each peg a couple of times, then pull them taut in direction of arrows as you tighten them. This method helps prevent slipping later.

When tuning, always tune *up* not down. **I**f you do tune the string too high and have to tune back down, tune string below required pitch *then* carefully tune back *up* to pitch. **S**trings may slip out of tune if tuned down to pitch. **D**on't put strings through the peg holes twice in an effort to secure them; they become too difficult to remove later.

See tip on tuning the instrument to itself (relative tuning) on page 15.

*Also by the same author: an Irish Traditional Music Book of 60 Tunes including some songs.
Six of the tunes are in this tutor.*

Please inquire at our Web site:

*http://www.irishmusictutor.com
or Email: info@irishmusictutor.com
or
The Publisher, or your local bookshop,
or C.C.E. Headquarters, Belgrave Square,
Monkstown, Co. Dublin
Ireland.
You can also contact the author through
C.C.E.*

CONCERT FLUTE / TIN WHISTLE
key-chart

The next few pages have the key-charts of a few commonly played instruments. These are included in the tutor to facilitate other members of families where more than one instrument is being learned.

Directly Below is the key-chart for the 'D' tin whistle. The Concert Flute is tuned the same as the 'D' whistle, so you can use the same diagram for both. Further below, the 'G' tin whistle. Sharp & flat notes other than those shown are played by only half opening the note hole.

D Whistle & Consort Flute Key Layout

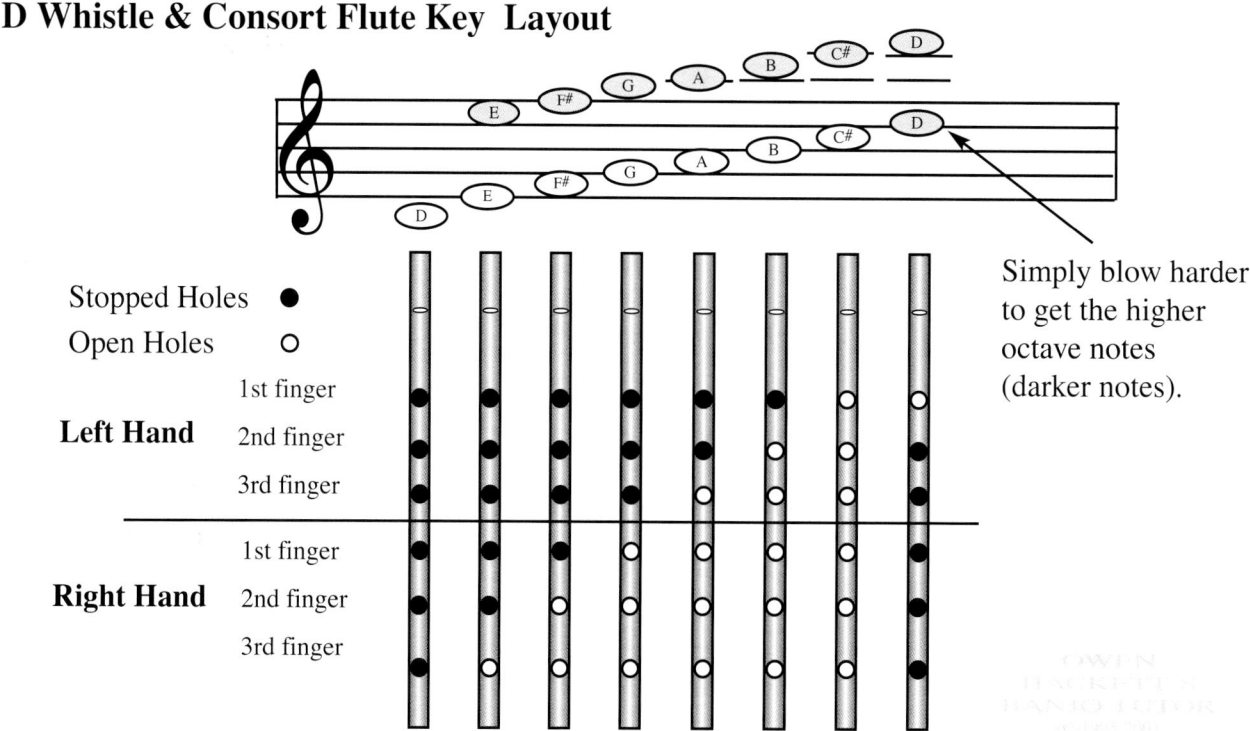

Simply blow harder to get the higher octave notes (darker notes).

G Whistle Key Layout

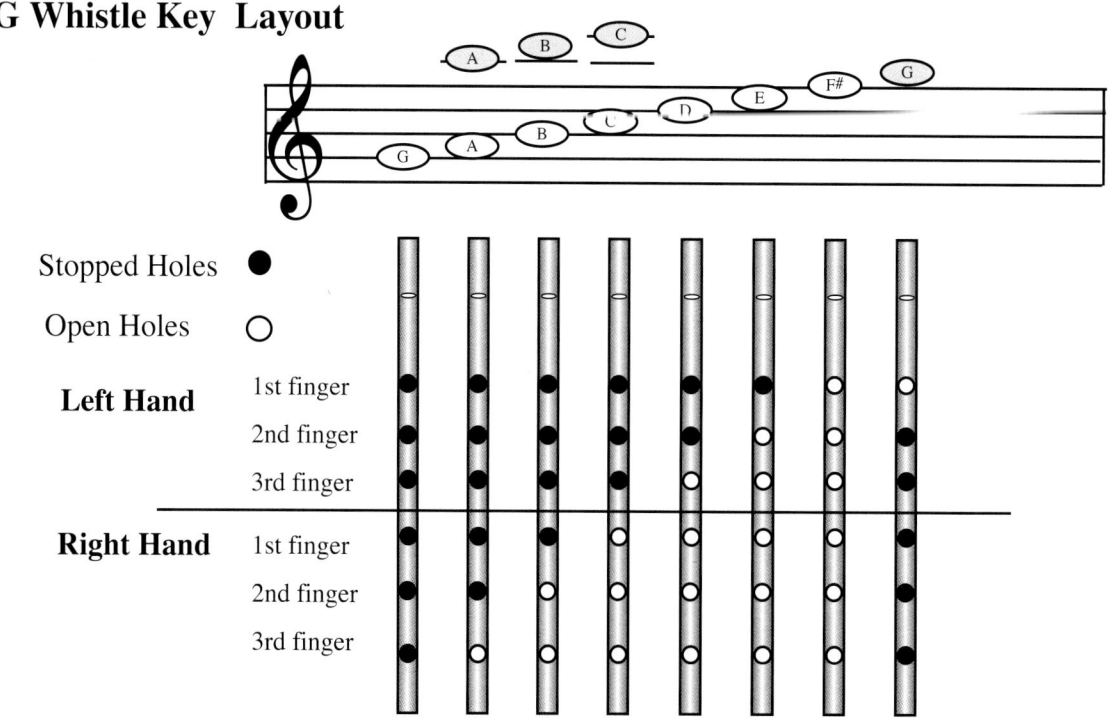

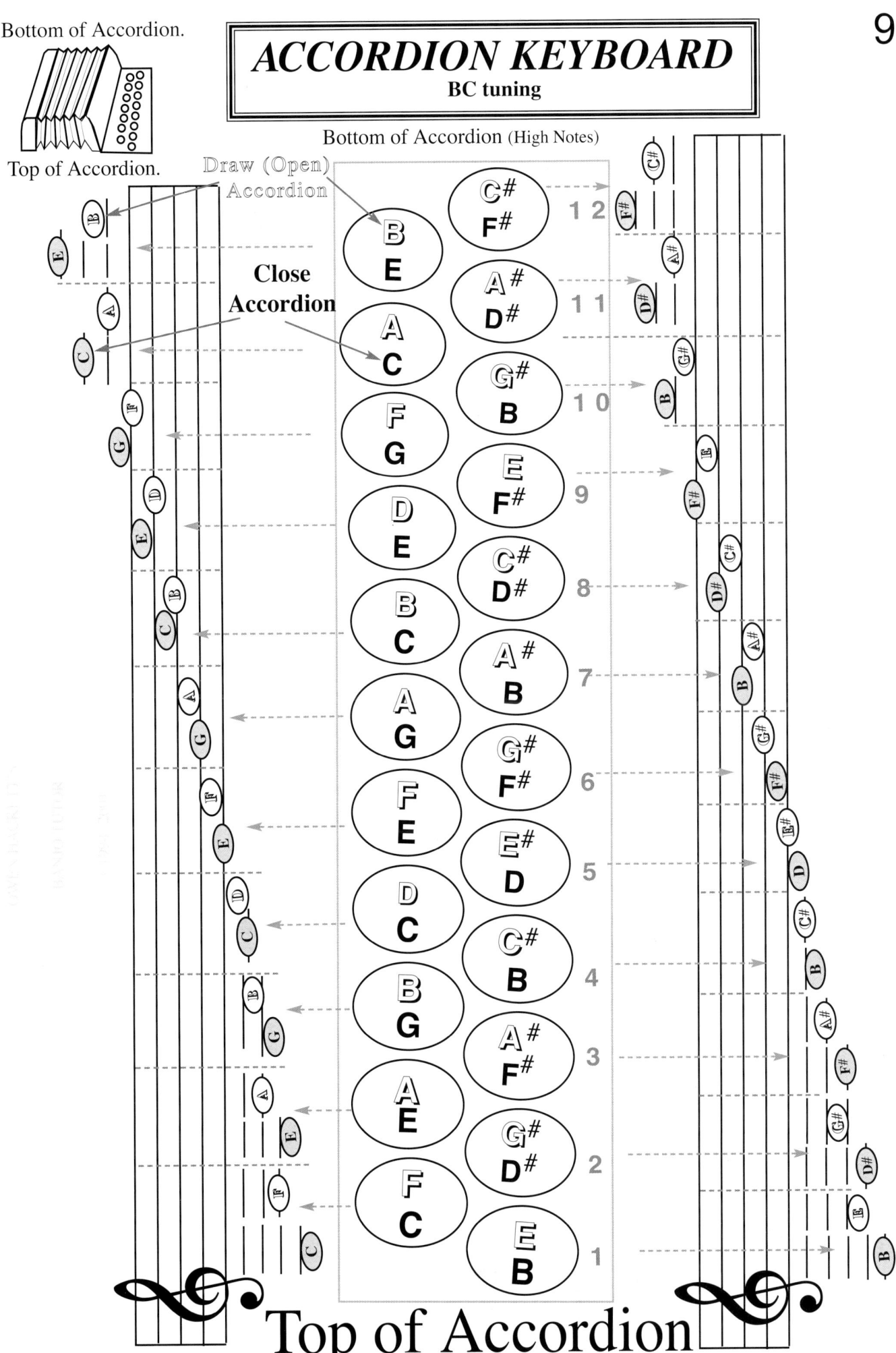

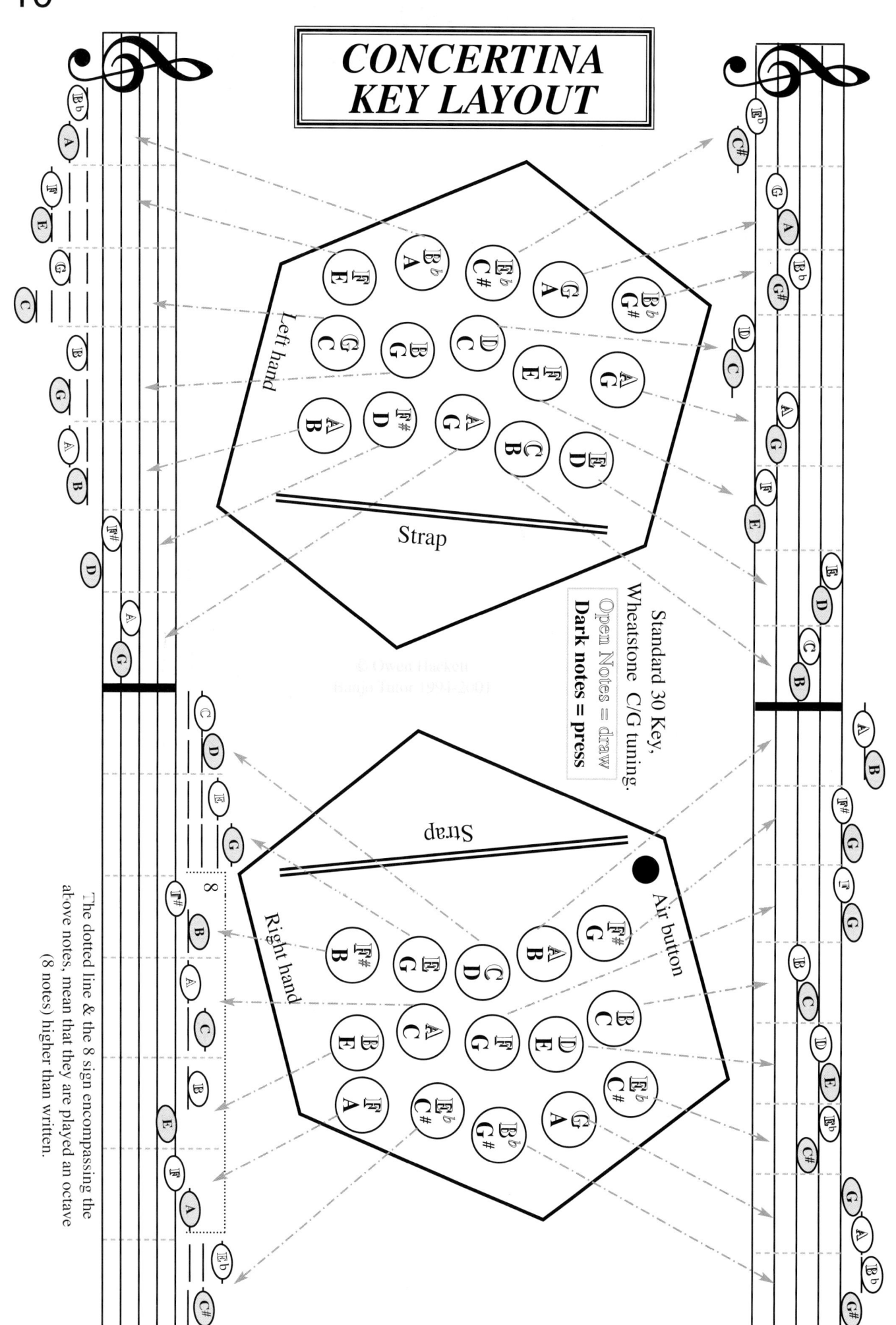

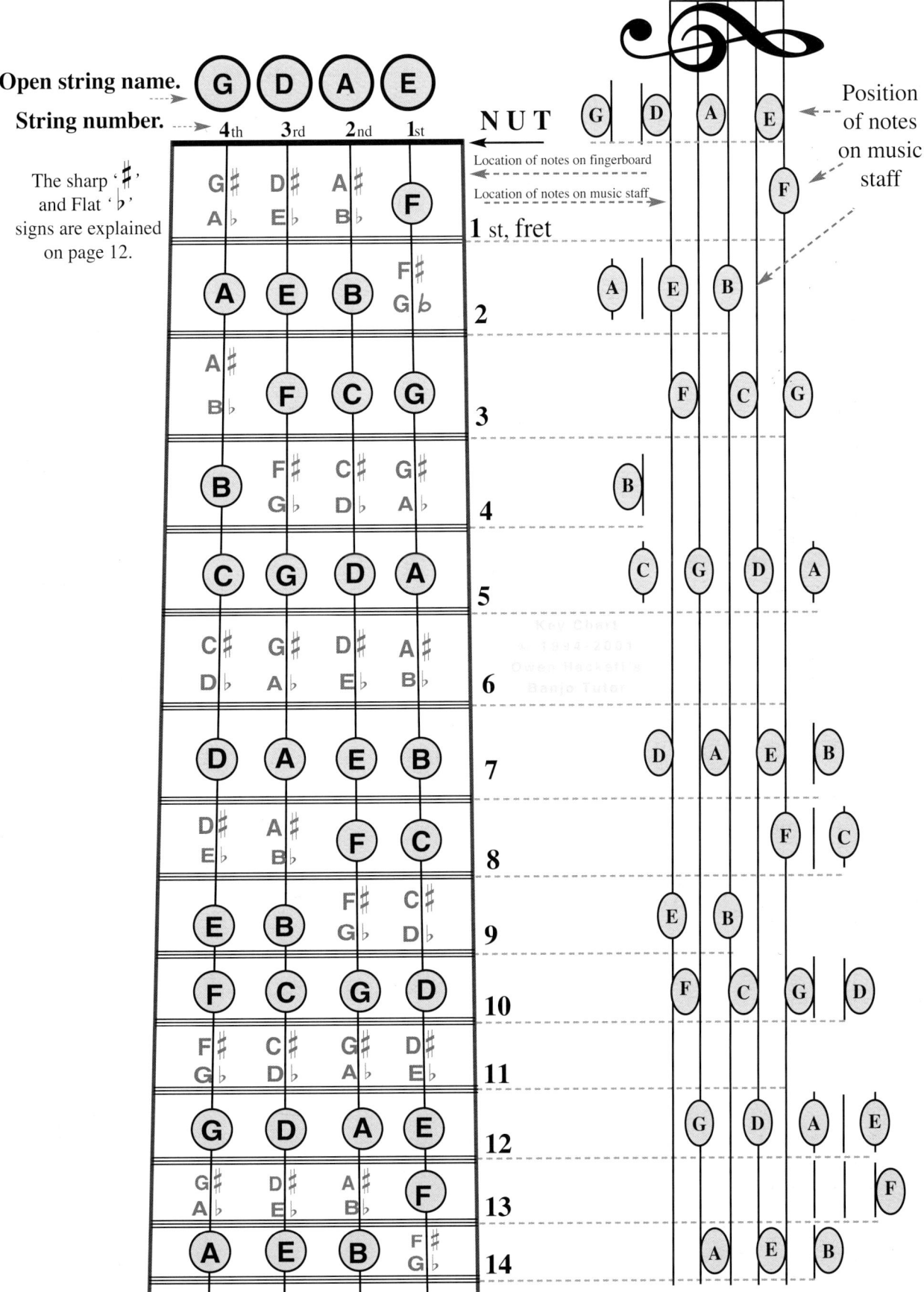

IMPORTANT STUFF

Before starting the actual lesson, it might be as well to familiarise ourselves with a few conventions and some of the elements we'll come across in the written music.

Don't feel intimidated by the contents of this page; simply use it as a reference page, where you can find a little help when needed.

These diagram five lines and four spaces is the Staff.

This fancy looking sign is the **treble** or *G* **clef**. When placed on the **staff**, it tells us the name of the notes on that staff. Notice how it circles around the second line fixing that line as *G*.

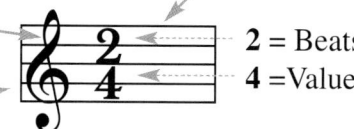

2 = Beats per bar
4 = Value of beats
IE. Two Crotchet beats.

Simple Duple Time.
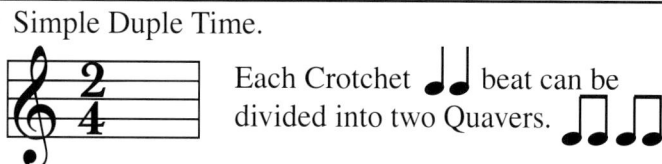
Each Crotchet beat can be divided into two Quavers.

Simple Triple Time
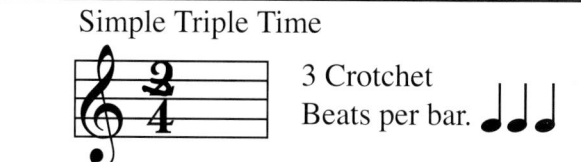
3 Crotchet Beats per bar.

Compound Duple Time.
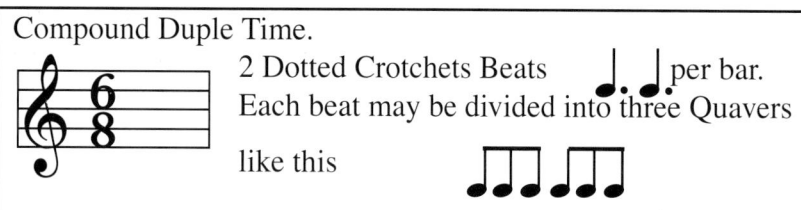
2 Dotted Crotchets Beats per bar. Each beat may be divided into three Quavers like this

Compound Triple Time
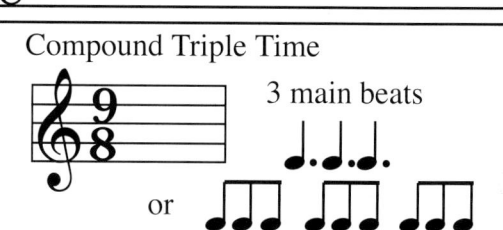
3 main beats

or

Simple Quadruple Time
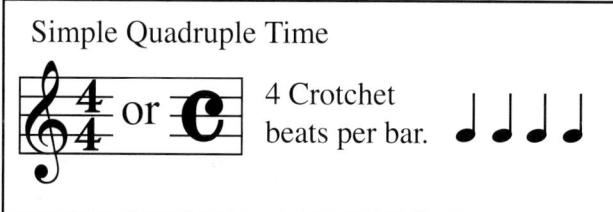
4 Crotchet beats per bar.

Compound Quadruple Time
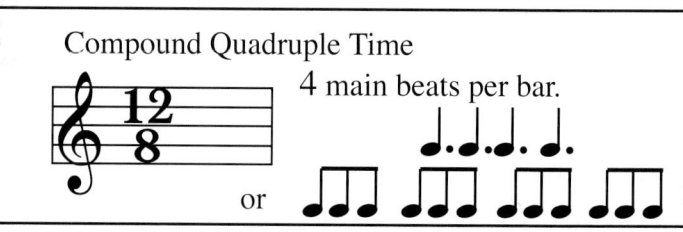
4 main beats per bar.

or

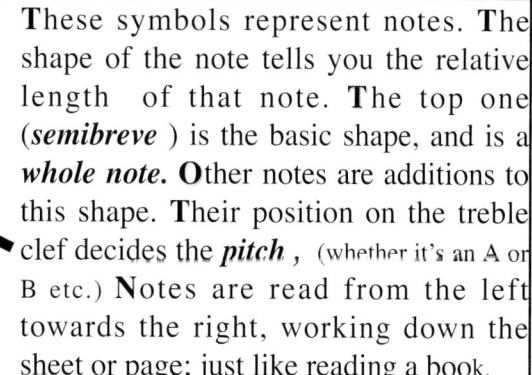

These symbols represent notes. The shape of the note tells you the relative length of that note. The top one (*semibreve*) is the basic shape, and is a *whole note.* Other notes are additions to this shape. Their position on the treble clef decides the *pitch*, (whether it's an A or B etc.) Notes are read from the left towards the right, working down the sheet or page; just like reading a book.

Note name	Shape	Rest	Relative Values
Semibreve	𝅝	𝄻	1 or Whole note
Minim	𝅗𝅥	𝄼	1/2 or Half note
Crotchet	♩	𝄽 or ↾	1/4 or Quarter Note
Quaver	♪	𝄾	1/8 or Eight Note
Semiquaver	𝅘𝅥𝅯	𝄿	1/16 or Sixteenth Nt.
Demisemiquaver	𝅘𝅥𝅰	𝅀	1/32 or Thirty second Note

Flagged Notes	Dotted Notes	Rests	Sharps	Flats	Naturals
♪ ← flag	♩.	See above.	♯	♭	♮
The value of a note is decreased by half for each flag placed on it. Like notes may be joined by, and have more than one flag.	The value of a note is increased by half when a dot is placed beside it. See Baidin Fheilimi.	Each note has it's equivalent rest sign. These signs are placed on the staff instead of a note when a period of silence is required. See Spancill Hill.	The *Sharp* sign is placed before a note to *raise* it one semitone (1 fret)	The *Flat* sign is placed before a note to *drop* it one semitone (1 fret)	The *Natural* sign is placed before a *sharpened* or *flattened* note to *restore* it to it's natural pitch.

There is more about these signs as we work through the tutor.

SCALES

13

Here are a few scales commonly found in Irish music.

G Major or E minor One sharp F.

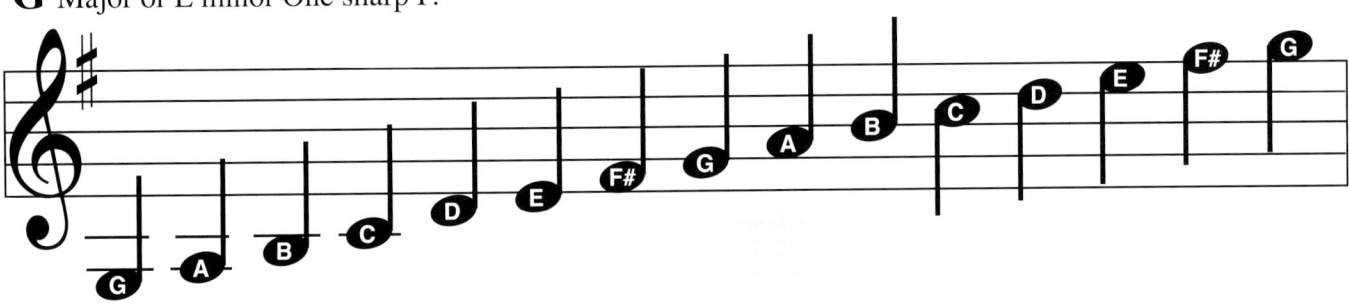

D Major or B minor Two sharps F; C.

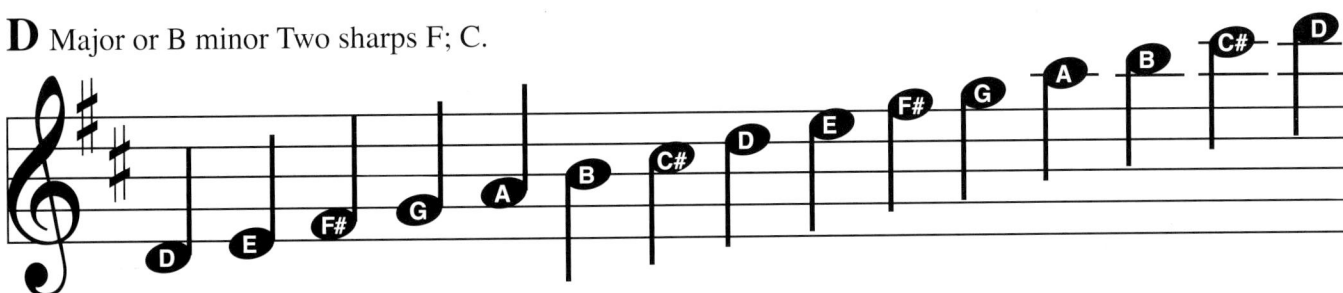

A Major or F minor. There are three sharpened notes. C; F; G.

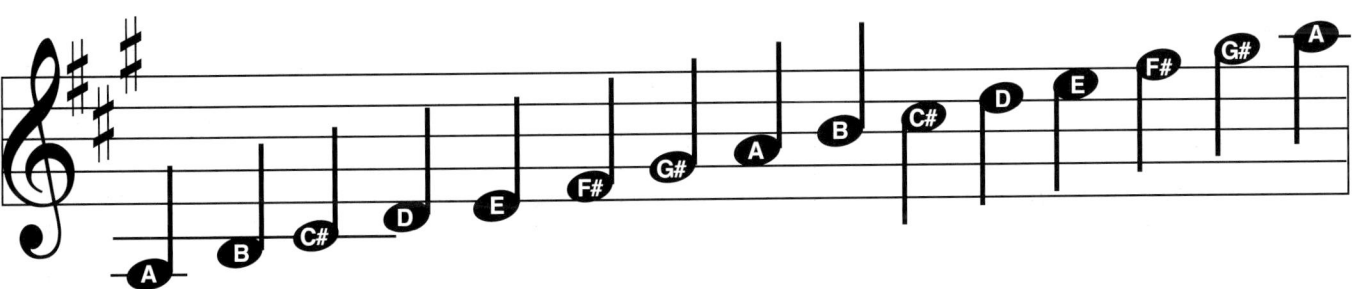

C Major or A minor. No sharpened or flattened notes.

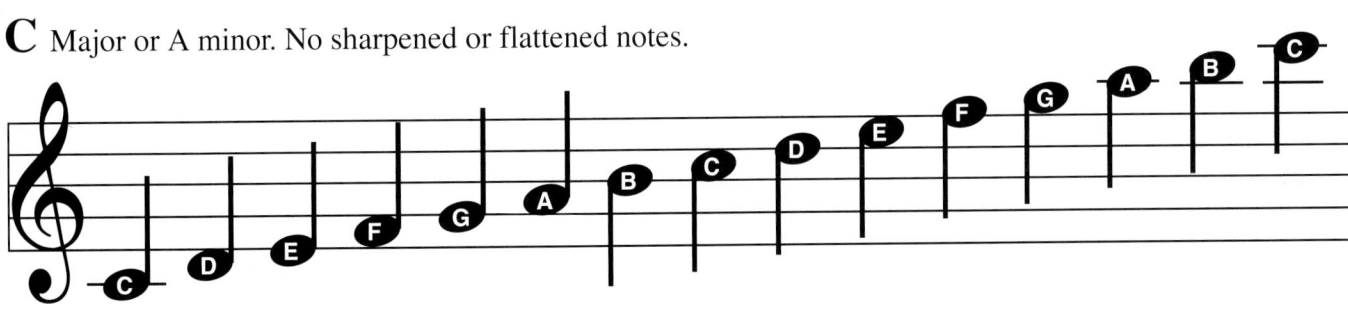

F Major or D minor. One flattened note. B

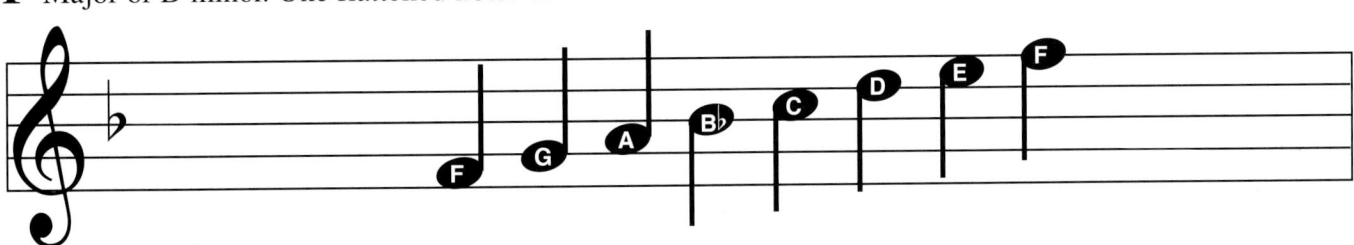

Notes below and above all these scales are also regularly used except for limitations set by a particular instrument. ie. G is the lowest note on the Violin or Banjo; (G scale above.) Etc....

BASIC EXERCISES

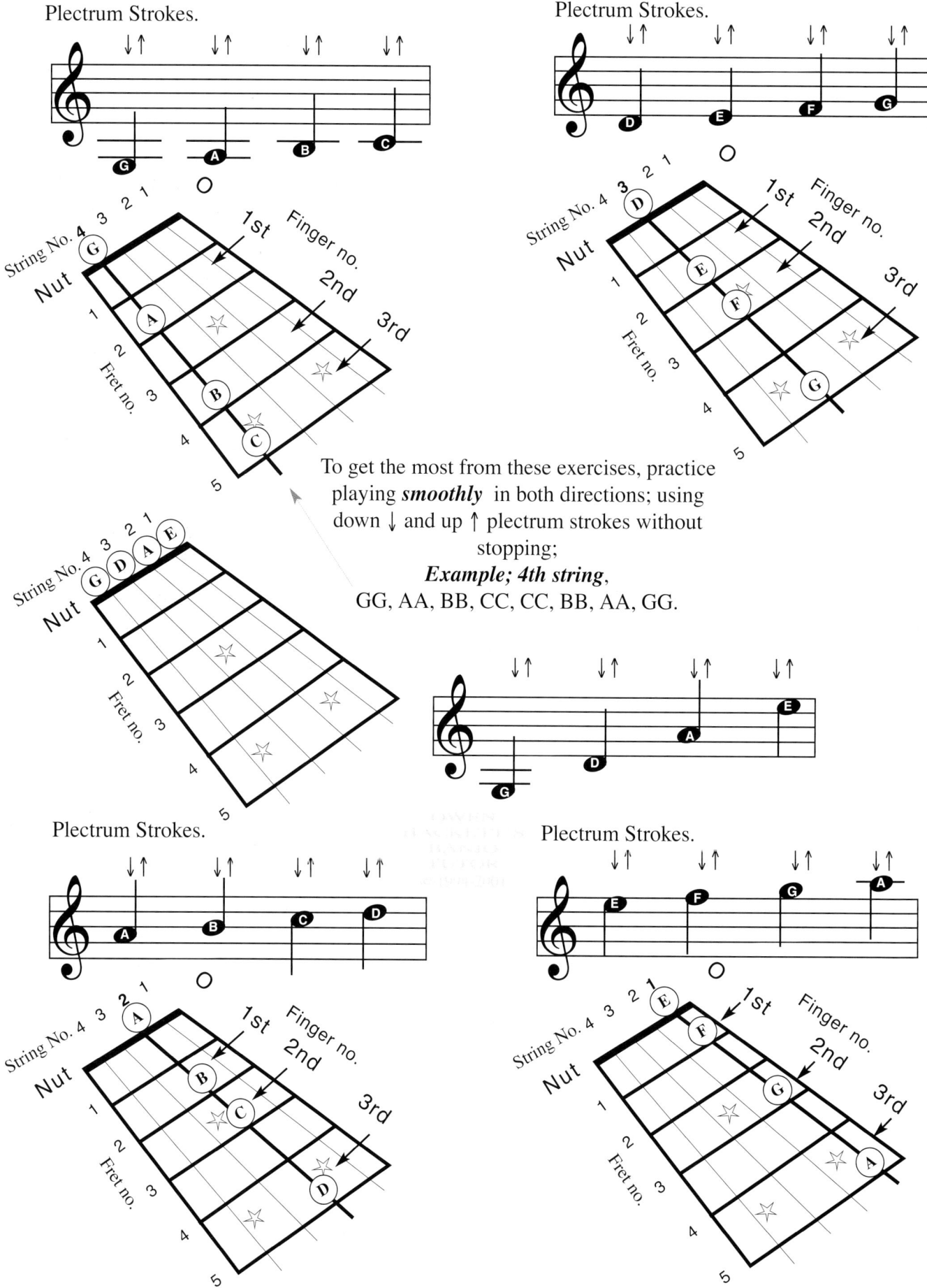

EXERCISE 1
PART 1

TWINKLE TWINKLE

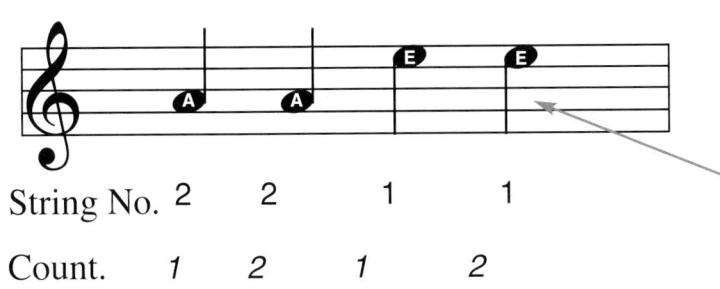

String No. 2   2   1   1
Count.   1   2   1   2

These first exercises are basic.
If you already have these basics, you might like to move on to the more advanced lessons.

Only the notes that appear on the treble clef appear on the instrument fingerboard diagram for easier location.

This exercise is designed to painlessly introduce the student to the position of the notes both on the banjo and the **treble clef** *(that's the five lines at the top of the page)*.

Making sure that the banjo is held in a comfortable position, hold the plectrum as described earlier and *gently* strike the **A** string away from you twice, while looking at the notes on the **treble clef** and noting their relevant position and names. Now do the same on the **E** string. *Repeat a number of times, naming the note as you play them.*

The notes you have just played are called **crotchets** or quarter note. These crotchets usually receive the count of *1*.

There are no fingers or frets used in this first exercise, Simply play the two open strings.

TIP; You can also use these notes to help tune your instrument. Start on lowest string and work your way towards the E. eg; (G-D;) (D-A;) (A-E.) Singing 'Twinkle Twinkle' or 'Ba Ba Black Sheep'(Next tune), for each pair. This actually helps train your ear for tuning the instrument to itself. Getting it up to **pitch** is a different story. Use a pitch pipes or a fixed note instrument for that for the moment.

To get the speed of the counting right, we'll assign one **second** to each **crotchet.** We'll write it like this;

♩ = 60. *meaning 60 crotchets per minute . (1 a second)*

If you like you could use the second hand on a watch or clock to assist you in counting evenly.

EXERCISE 1
PART 2

TWINKLE TWINKLE.

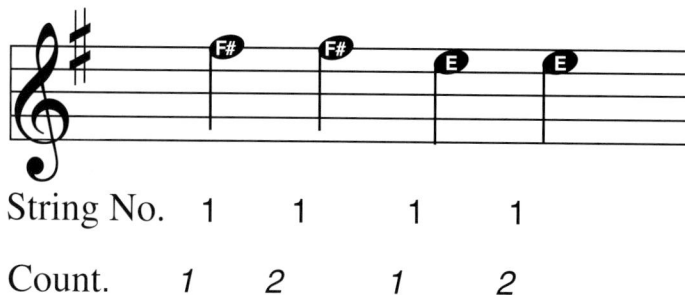

String No.   1   1   1   1
Count.   1   2   1   2

This time we'll introduce the first finger. If you look at the fingerboard, you will see that the finger is placed just behind the 2nd fret. on the 1st string. This gives **F sharp** (F♯) When a note is played sharp, it simply means that the natural note, (F, in this case,) has been raised up one fret, or *semitone*

IMPORTANT

The key signature, ie: names of notes, ♯'s & ♭'s are shown on the actual notes only in this tutor. It is usually only written at the beginning of the treble clef, like this.

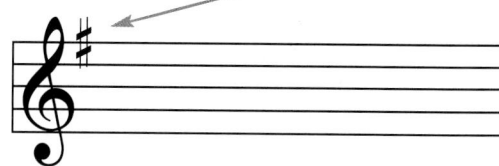

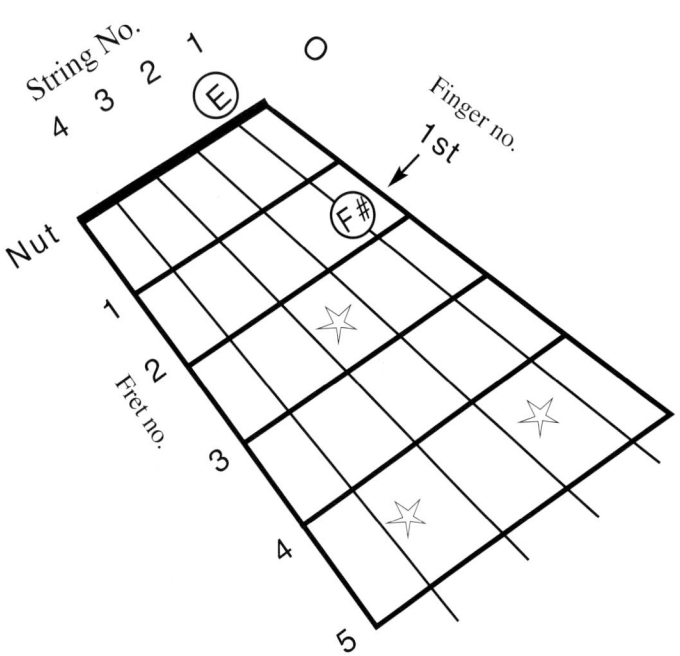

Remember to always check the key signature signs before you start a tune. *All the notes* on the line or space which bears the ♯ sign, will be raised **one semi-tone** (one fret) We will be adding some more ♯'s on the treble clef in the next lesson.

Don't forget to point your fingers back along the fretboard.

Note position of thumb.

Hold the plectrum lightly between thumb and first finger, allowing it to *glide* over the strings.

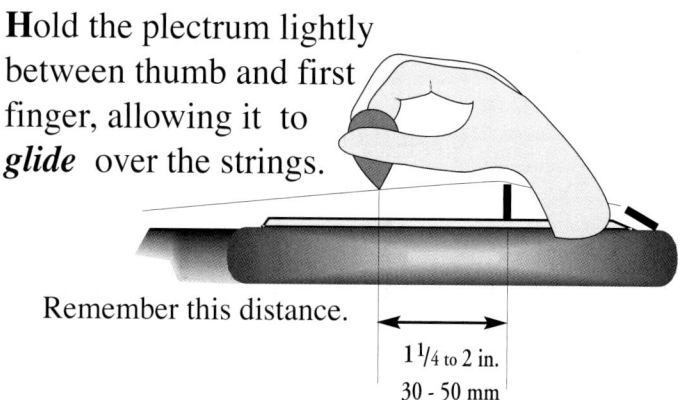

Remember this distance.

1 1/4 to 2 in.
30 - 50 mm

EXERCISE 1
PART 3

TWINKLE TWINKLE.

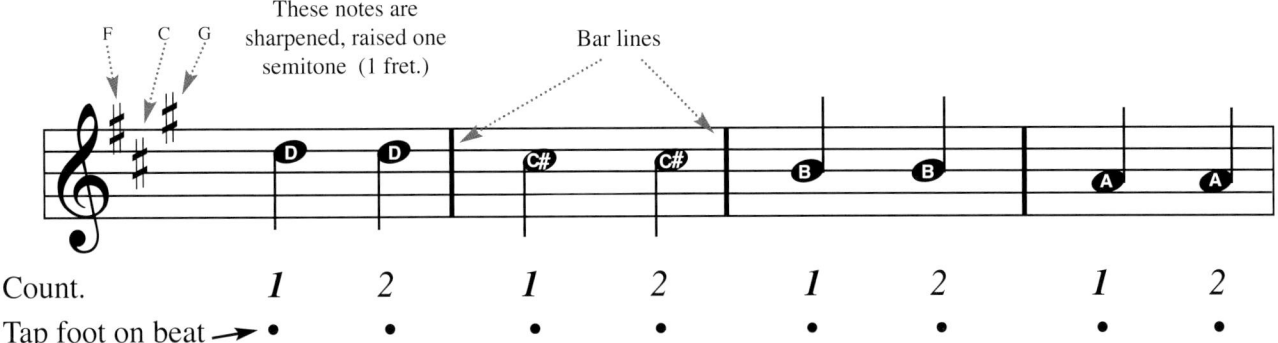

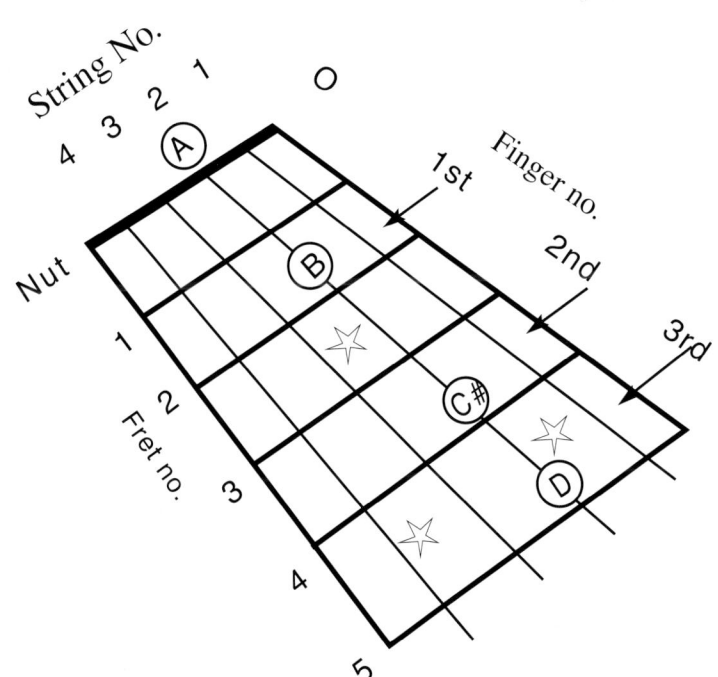

You will have noticed that some vertical lines have been added to the treble clef at the top of the page. These are called *bar-lines* and are put into the staff to divide the music into *equal* measures or beats. When you listen to music, you will notice that there is a steady *beat* that you could clap your hands or tap your foot to. The *strongest* of these beats are called *Accents* and usually fall on the first note of each *bar.*

We have now a second sharp note C♯ which is played by placing the 2nd finger on the 2nd string, on the 4th fret.

It is very important that you use the proper fingering as shown in the diagrams.

Now repeat the above lesson a few times. don't forget to tap your foot on the main beat at the *beginning* of each *bar, where the count says 1.*

If you like you may tap also at the 2nd count, although some players omit this.

Don't forget to keep the notes evenly spaced out; about one second each.

Now play the all three parts as one.

Please read through each lesson fully, before attempting it. Doing so will make it much easier to learn.

EXERCISE 1
PART 4

TWINKLE TWINKLE.

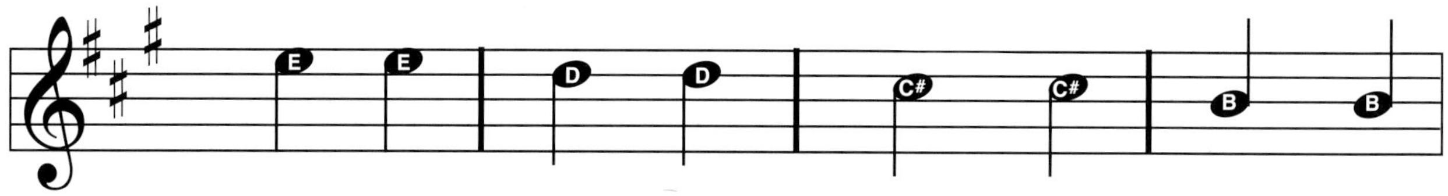

[Music staff: E E | D D | C# C# | B B]

Count.   1   2   1   2   1   2   1   2
Tap foot on beat   •   •   •   •   •   •   •   •

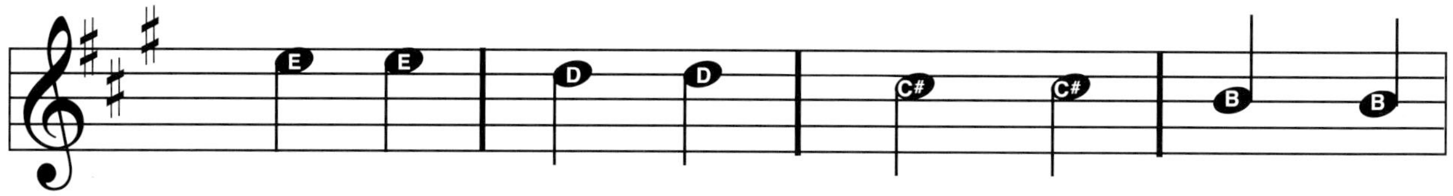

[Music staff: E E | D D | C# C# | B B]

Count.   1   2   1   2   1   2   1   2
Tap foot on beat   •   •   •   •   •   •   •   •

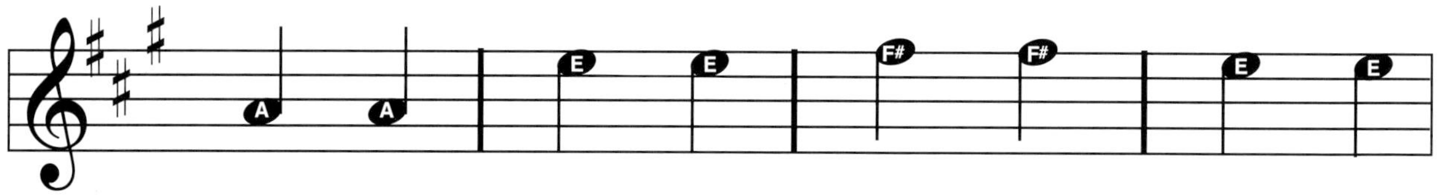

[Music staff: A A | E E | F# F# | E E]

Count.   1   2   1   2   1   2   1   2
Tap foot on beat   •   •   •   •   •   •   •   •

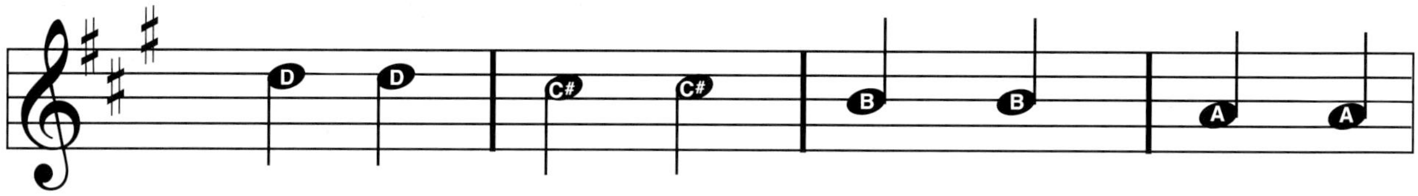

[Music staff: D D | C# C# | B B | A A]

Count.   1   2   1   2   1   2   1   2
Tap foot on beat   •   •   •   •   •   •   •   •

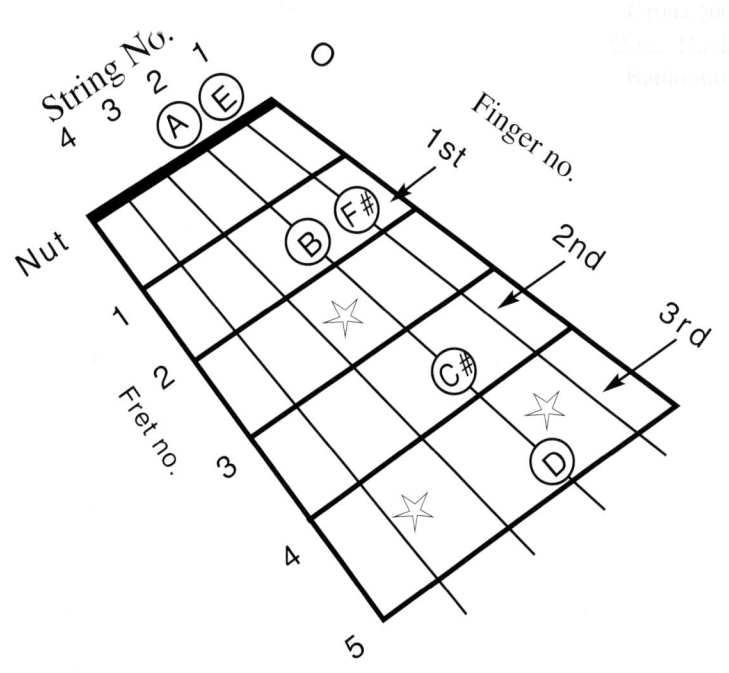

In this lesson, there are more music staves on the page but you are familiar with all the notes. **T**ry playing them all and don't forget to tap your foot at the **beginning** of each **bar**. *(Where the count says **1**).*
We'll be using *time signatures* in lesson 3.

EXERCISE 2
PART 1

BAA BAA BLACK SHEEP.

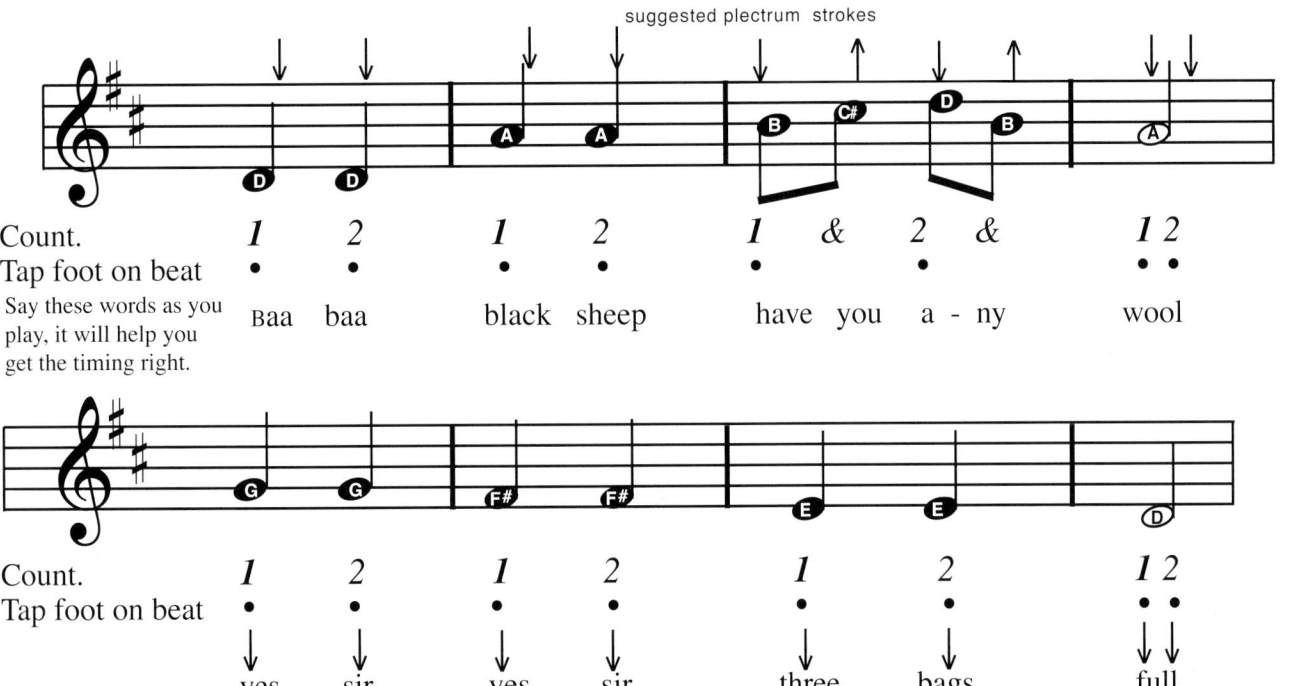

Count. 1 2 | 1 2 | 1 & 2 & | 1 2
Tap foot on beat

Say these words as you play, it will help you get the timing right.

Baa baa | black sheep | have you a-ny | wool

Count. 1 2 | 1 2 | 1 2 | 1 2
Tap foot on beat

yes sir, | yes sir, | three bags | full

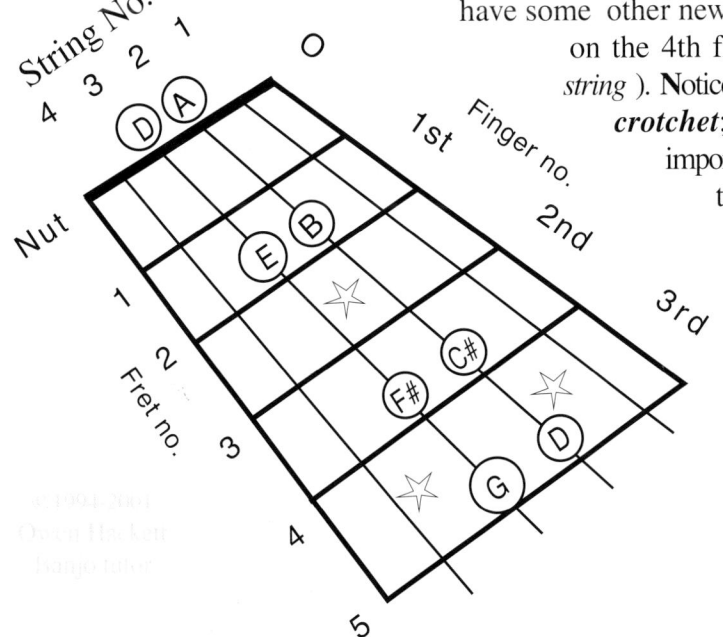

In this 2nd exercise we begin on the 3rd string ***D***. D**on't confuse this *D* with the higher *D* you played in the last lesson. Y**ou also have some other new notes to learn. The ***G*** on the 5th fret; ***F*** ♯ on the 4th fret; and ***E*** on the 2nd fret, (*all on the 3rd string*). Notice there are **3** different lengths of notes. *minim*; *crotchet*; and *quaver*. T**o get them right, it is very important to get the counting right. T**ake your time, tapping your foot on *each* count of **1**. P**lay the notes evenly, fitting them smoothly into the counting.

Think of the words as you play the notes, and singing the counting, ie, 1-2; 1-2; 1 & 2 &-; etc. You should, (with practice) be able to get the timing and note values correct. The direction that you move the plectrum is shown by the little arrows. The **down** arrow ↓ (towards the ground) - The **up** arrow ↑ (towards your head).

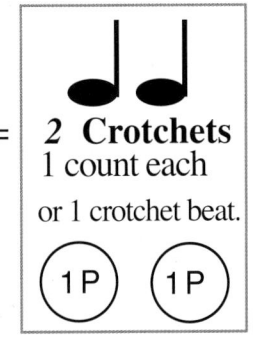

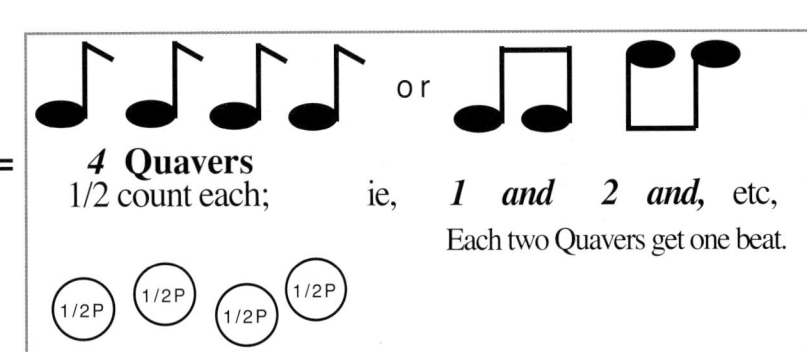

EXERCISE 2
PART 2

BAA BAA BLACK SHEEP.

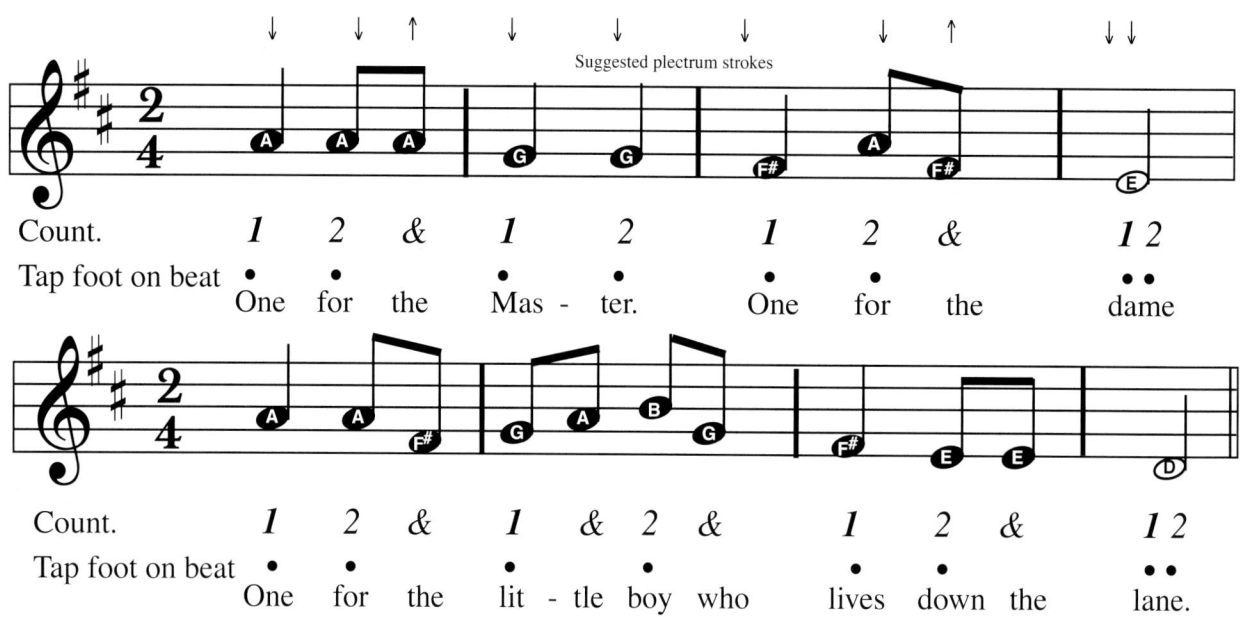

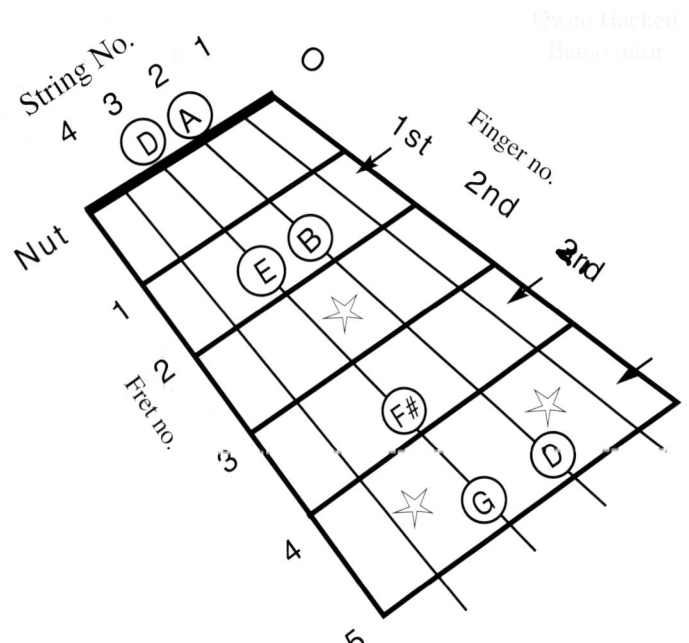

The most confusing part of any lesson for a beginner, is trying to learn everything at once.

Don't worry too much about the little directional arrows for the plectrum. They are simply a guide. Most players tend to work out the proper strokes fine on their own with a little practice.

Just remembering to hit the next string in the same direction you were moving to get to that string in the first place, will keep you on the right track.

Did you notice the two ♯ sharp signs at the beginning of the tune? **F♯** and **C♯** They tell us that the tune is in the key of **D**. All the F and C notes in this tune are sharpened one semitone. (Raised one fret).

minim is a 1/2 note and for the moment we'll give it a count of two.

crotchet is a 1/4 note (2 to a minim) and receives a count of one.

quaver is a 1/8 note and receives a 1/2 count. ie. *two quavers* to the *one* count.

To be able to get the counting right, count like this; (**1 and**). By saying (*and*) it helps divide the count evenly.

EXERCISE 3
PART 1

JINGLE BELLS

Our third tune in $\frac{2}{4}$ time, is in polka tempo.

You might also like to say '**&**' between these notes until you master the rhythm

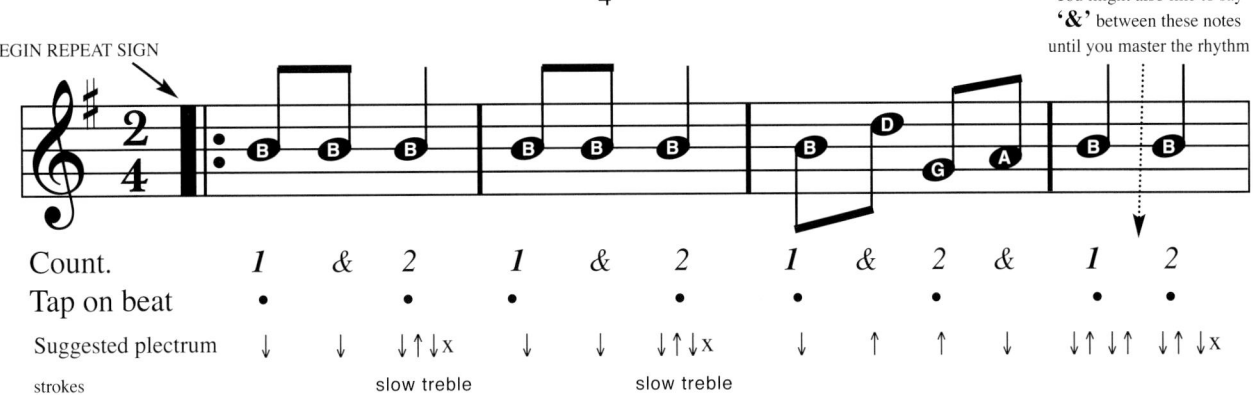

Most tunes are repeated at least once. The first time around, the ending notes are written so as to give a suggestion of continuance. This makes the listener feel the tune is going to continue and not end there. These notes are given the 1st ending sign ⌐1.⌐ indicating that they are to be played the first time around.

When you come to these notes the second time around, you skip over them and play the notes indicated by the second time around sign.⌐2.⌐ These second time around notes may differ only very slightly from the first ones, but are written so as to give a feeling of finality to the tune.

See next page.

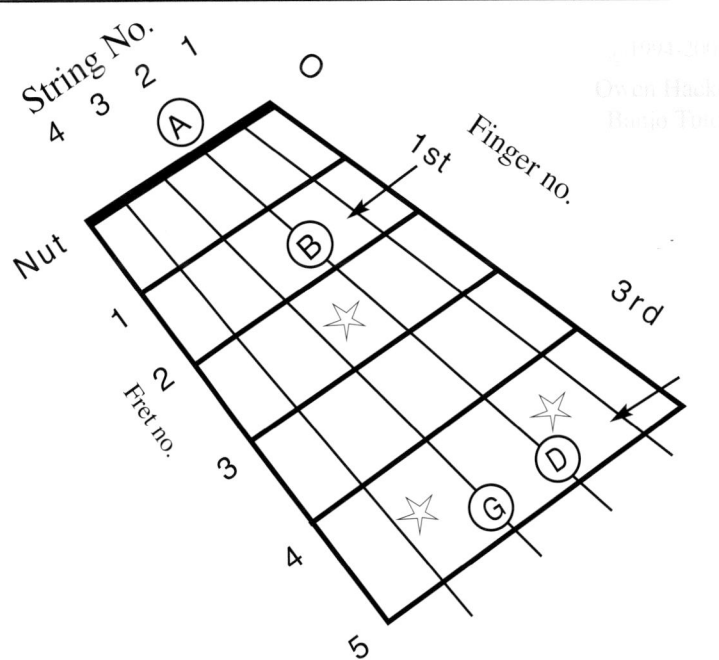

In a polka, **both** counts receive a strong emphasis, while the notes in between the 1 & 2 don't. It will help a lot, if you tap your foot on **both** counts.

The one sharp ♯ is F. This means all the F's in the tune are sharpened, raised one semitone or fret. The tune is in the key of G.

In order to give the first note of each bar that little extra emphasis, I like to omit the very last plectrum stroke of the preceding note, and play what could be called a slow treble ↓↑↓x The X stands for the omitted stroke. Beginners might find this a little bit difficult to grasp, but it does work very well in practice.

As in speech, music also has phrases. The following instructions will endeavour to illustrate this. First read the upper line aloud, then the lower line, to the same tempo.

UPPER LINE ;	Jin - gle bells,	jin - gle bells,	jin - gle all the	w a y.
LOWER LINE ;	1 *and* 2;	1 *and* 2,	1 *and* 2 *and*	1 2.

If you have phrased the words properly, and the counting to the same tempo, you will find that the '*and*' divides the count of *1 - 2* in half.

Please remember to keep to the correct fingering, no matter how difficult.

EXERCISE 3
PART 2

JINGLE BELLS

Now play the whole tune

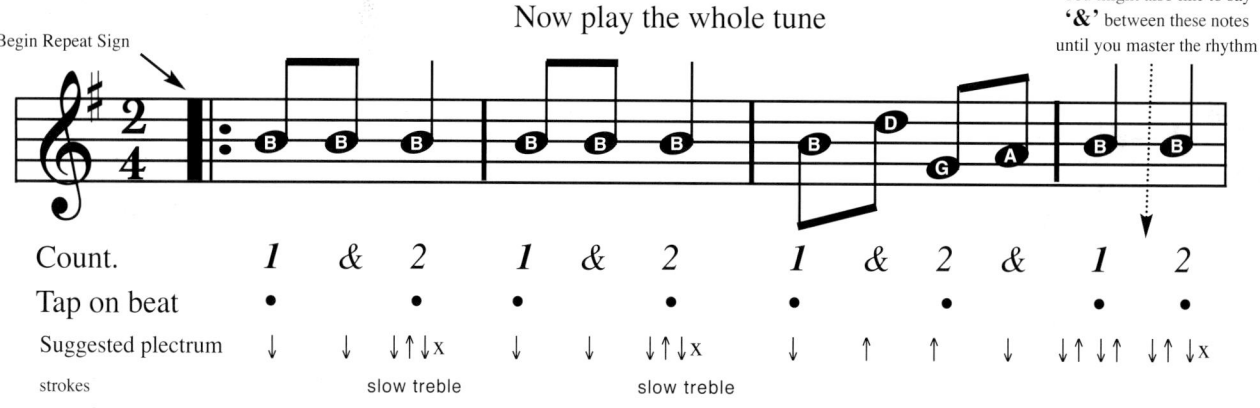

JINGLE BELLS

Play this section first time round, then go back to start again, skip over this section and play section underneath 2nd time.

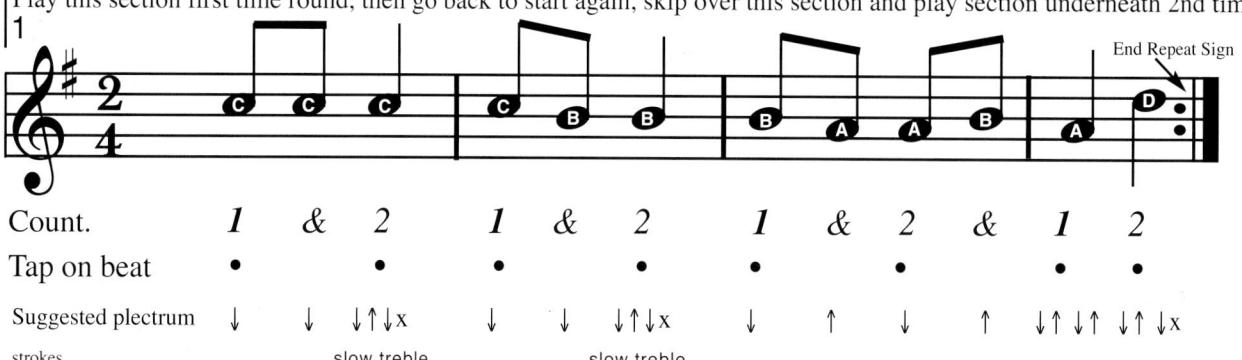

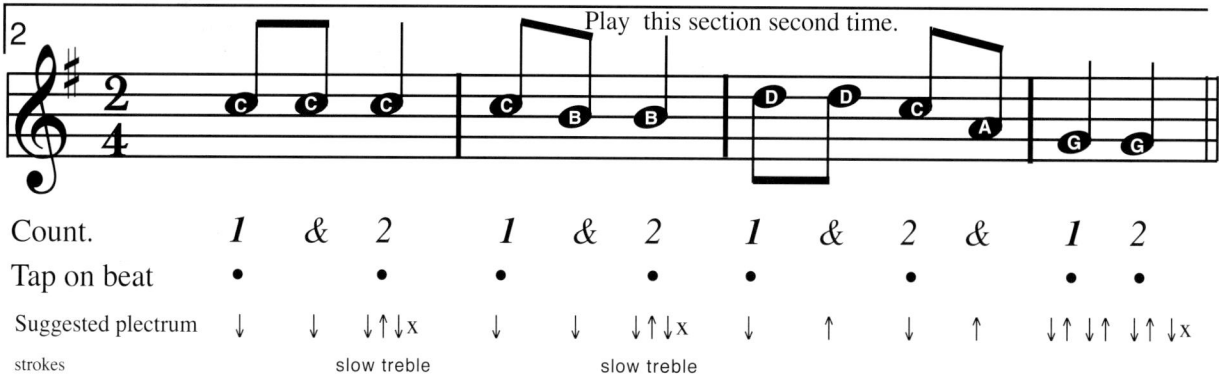

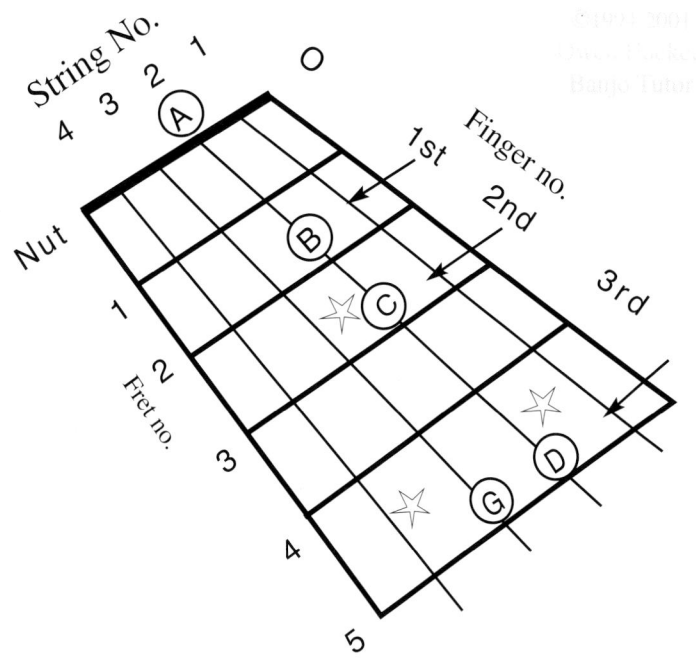

In this polka, we have three different combinations of notes, making up two crotchets per bar, ie $\frac{2}{4}$ time.

Bars 1 and 2 have a crotchet ♩ and two quavers ♪♪ or ♫ Bar 3 has four Quavers. And bar 4 has two Crotchets.

For very slow music, the crotchet ♩ should receive four alternating down ↓ and up ↑ strokes. This would only be suitable for an instrument playing a very rapid tremolo. But in faster music, the crotchet gets two ↓↑ strokes.

It sometimes could be played as a triplet. And in some tunes it could be played once and held for it's duration. You will see this later in the tutor.

EXERCISE 3
PART 3

JINGLE BELLS

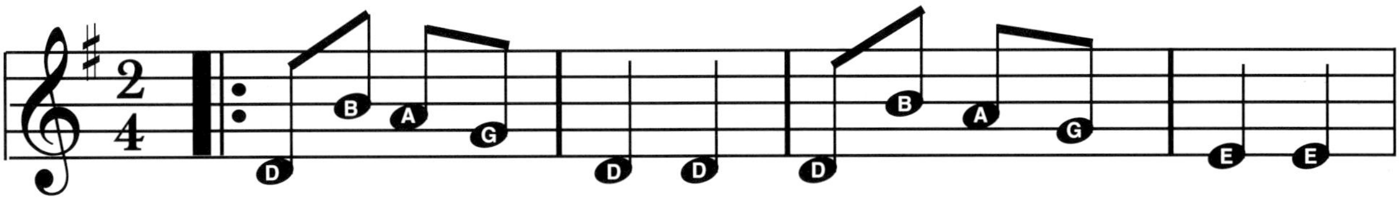

(Music notation - Part 1)

Count.	1	&	2	&	1	2	1	&	2	&	1	2
Tap on beat	•	•	•	•	•	•	•	•	•	•	•	•

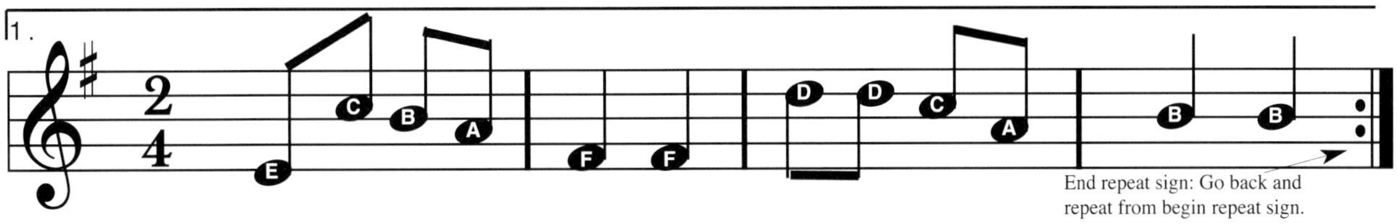

(Music notation - 1st ending)

End repeat sign: Go back and repeat from begin repeat sign.

Count.	1	&	2	&	1	2	&	1	&	2	&	1	2
Tap on beat	•	•	•	•	•	•	•	•	•	•	•	•	•

(Music notation - 2nd ending)

Lead-in note; use when repeating the tune a 2nd time

Double bar: Marks end of piece or section

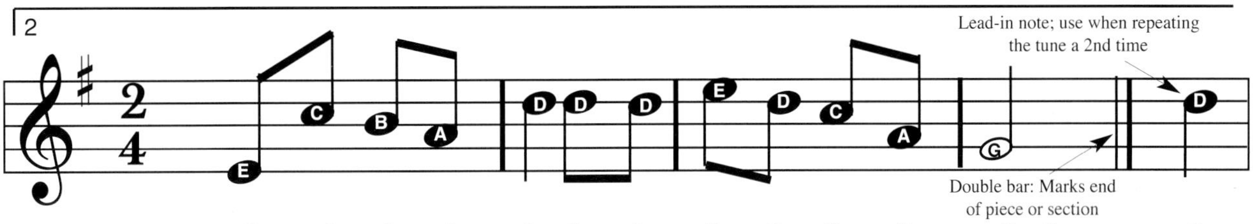

Count.	1	&	2	&	1	2	&	1	&	2	&	1	2	1
Tap on beat	•	•	•	•	•	•	•	•	•	•	•	•	•	•

REPEAT SIGNS

At the start of the polka, you see a new sign like this; ‖: It is a **begin repeat sign.** Further on in the music, you see another sign :‖ This is an **end repeat sign.** When you encounter an **end repeat sign**, you must go back from that point, and repeat what is written between the two signs.

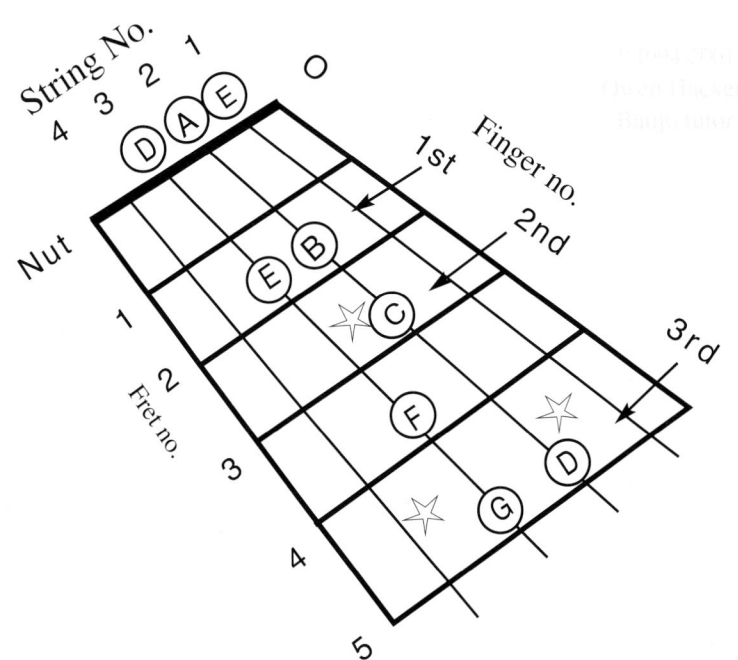

On the fretboard, the fingers must press down the strings **close behind** the fret in order to produce a clear note. Practice extending and flexing your fingers even when not playing the banjo. This helps to make them more supple and flexible. Make sure to use proper fingering as indicated.

EXERCISE 4

ROW ROW ROW YOUR BOAT.

This tune will help you, in learning to play different note values correctly. Think of the words in your mind as you play. Note that each Triplet occupies a crotchet space.

LONDON BRIDGE.

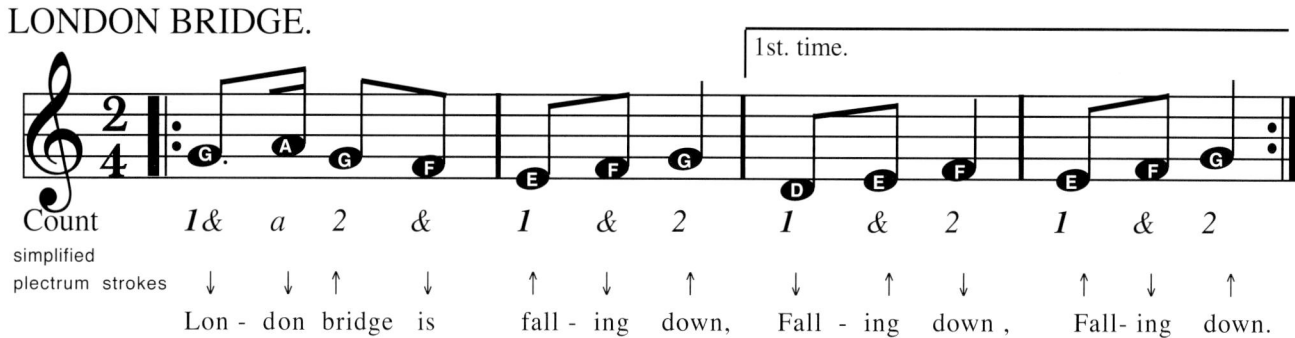

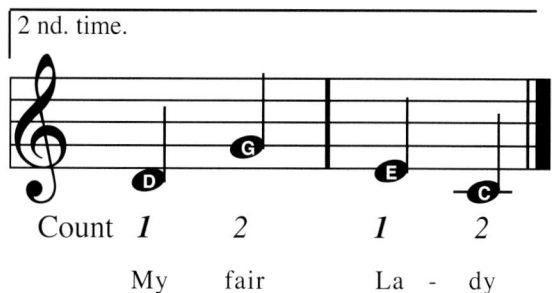

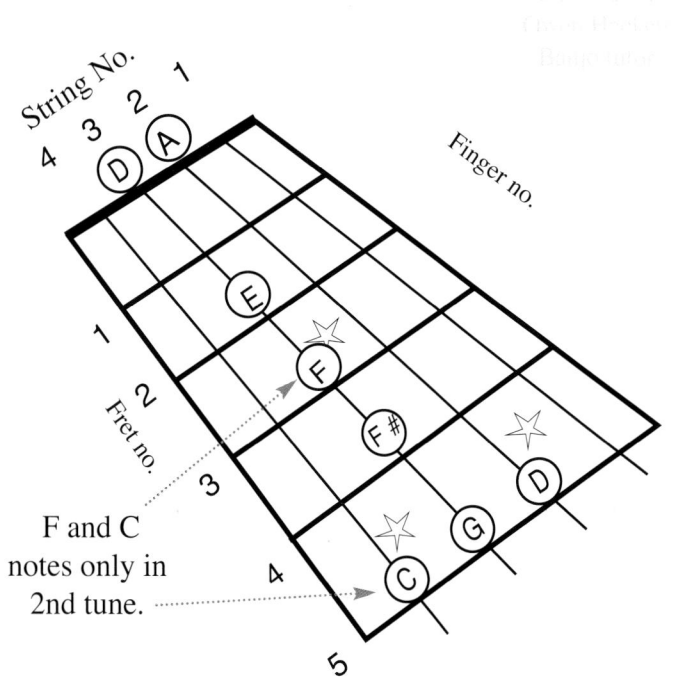

F and C notes only in 2nd tune.

Here we have two little tunes in the keys of D and C. If you carefully follow the instructions for the top one, you should be able to apply what you learn to the 2nd one. Remember! don't rush any of these practice lessons. It's much better to play the melody at a nice steady rhythm.

EXERCISE 5
PART 1

BAIDIN FHEILIMI

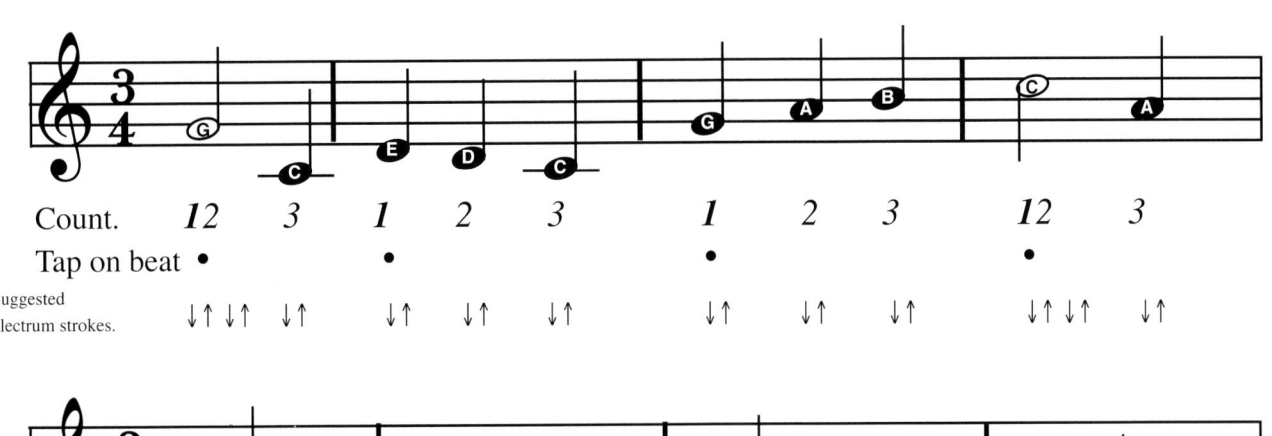

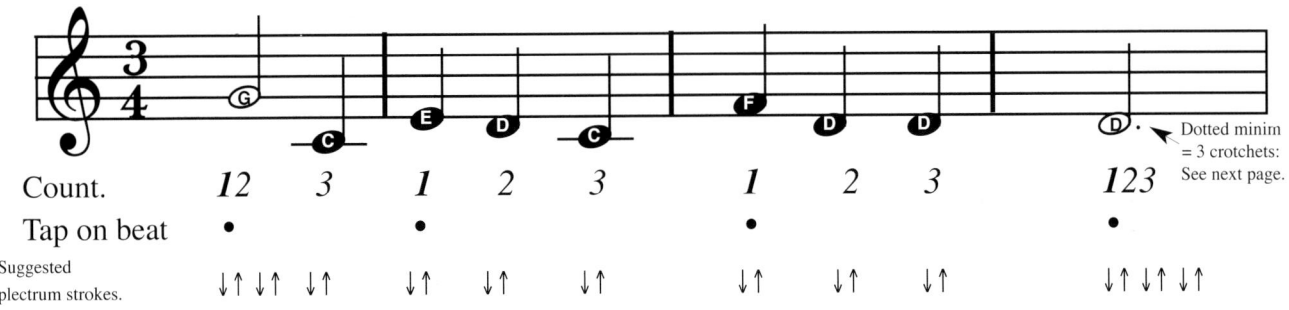

Dotted minim = 3 crotchets: See next page.

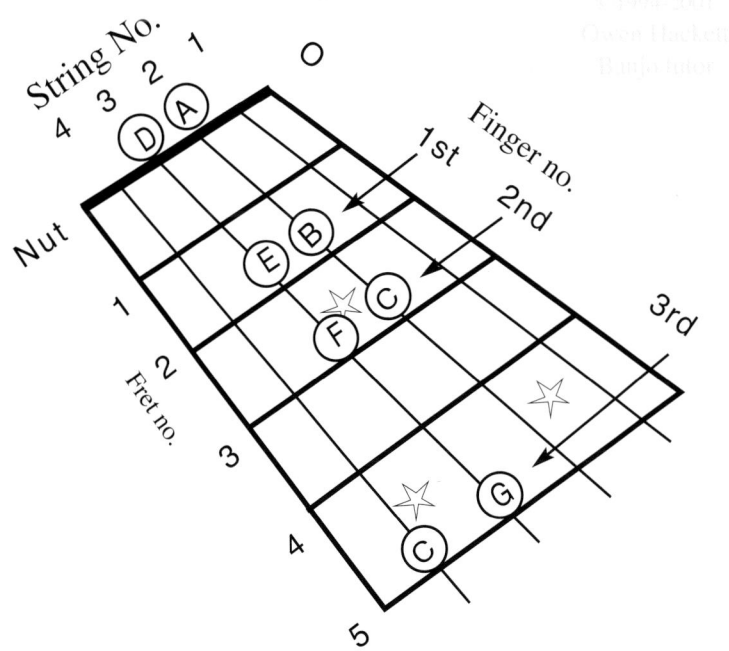

In exercise 5 we have a new rhythm to learn, 3/4 or waltz time in the key of C. We have to be very accurate with the plectrum.

First practice counting aloud
1-2-3; **1**-2-3; **1**-2-3.

Then get into a steady down ↓ and up ↑ rhythm. Striking any one string down ↓↑ on the count of **1**; then ↓↑ for the **2** etc.

Try and develop a smooth flowing rhythm as you practice.

Counting **1**-2-3; **1**-2-3; over and over, and emphasising the **1** each time, practice the following exercise by striking the strings until you have mastered the technique. Do ↓↑ three times on the 1st. string. Change smoothly to the 2nd. string, then the 3rd. and the 4th. Then work your way smoothly back to the 1st. string. Remember that even though you are only counting to 3, you are supposed to strike the strings 6 times.

↓↑ for 1; ↓↑ for 2; and ↓↑ for 3. **Initially**, you might like to say *AND* between the counting, ie (↓**1**)(↑*and*)(↓**2**)(↑*and*)(↓**3**)(↑*and*) etc.

EXERCISE 5
PART 2

BAIDIN FHEILIMI

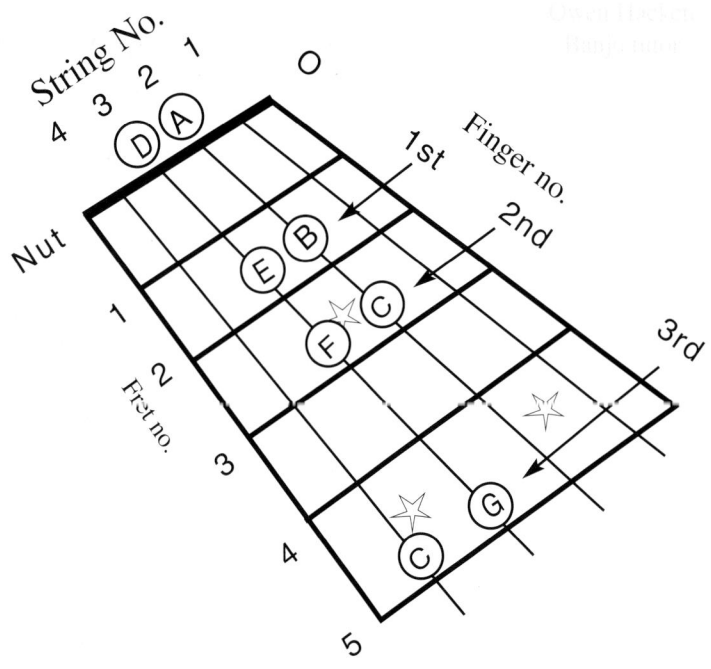

The little lines that you see below the staff (above, and previous page) are **leger lines**. These leger lines are used when the notes are lower or higher in pitch than the five line staff allow. Remember, the tune is in the key of C. That is the F and C notes are not sharpened. These are called C natural and F natural. Note their positions on the fingerboard.

The dot following the white half note (minim) gives it the new value of a 3/4 note. So instead of it getting ↓↑ ↓↑, (a count of 2); it now gets ↓↑ ↓↑ ↓↑ (a count of 3).

At first, you might experience difficulty fingering the changing notes without disrupting the rhythm of the plectrum and music. One way to overcome this, is to pick any one or two bars you like, (ones that have notes you find easy to get.) Work on these until you are able to change from note to note smoothly.

EXERCISE 5
PART 3

BAIDIN FHEILIMI

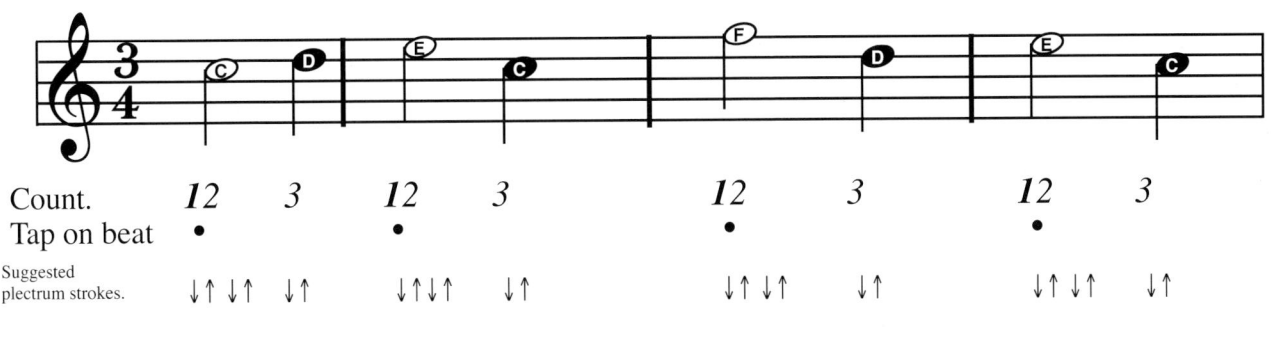

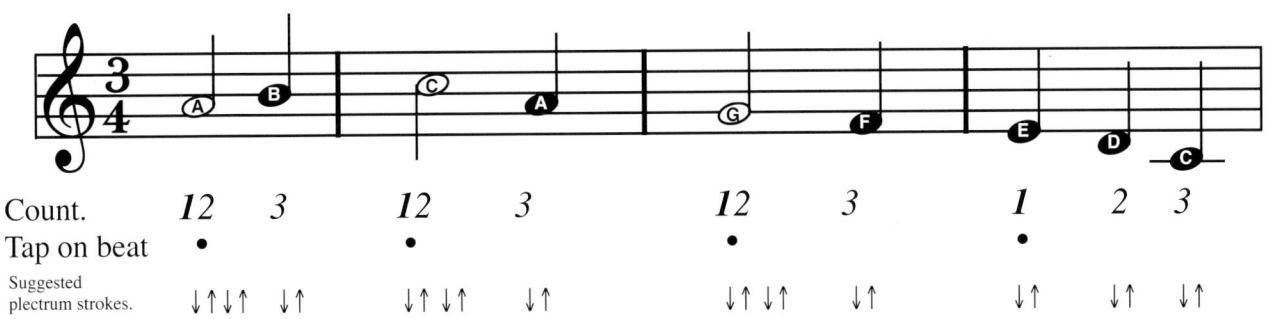

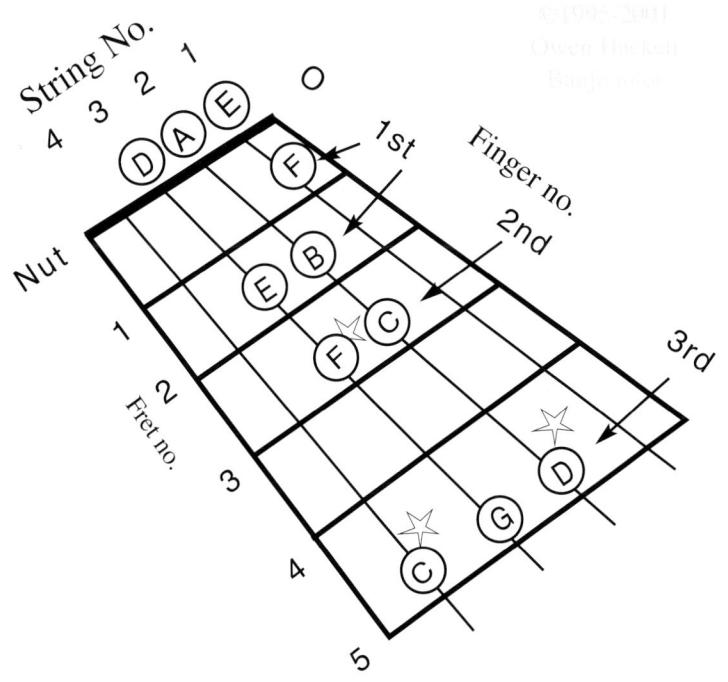

At the bottom of the page you will find some help for getting the counting right.

Remember to hold the plectrum *lightly,* letting it glide over the strings rather than plucking hard. This will require a good bit of practice to prevent it slipping from between your fingers. But if you persevere, the overall quality of your music will greatly improve including the tone from the instrument.

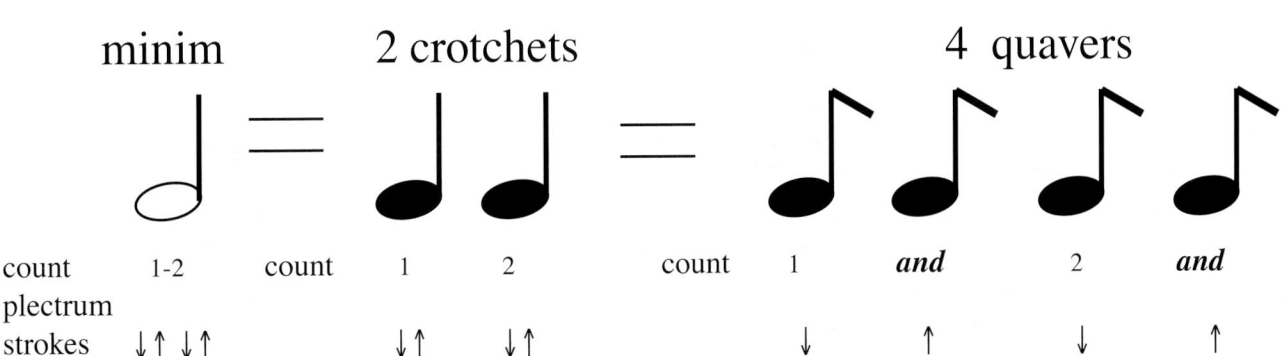

EXERCISE 5
PART 4

BAIDIN FHEILIMI

There is a large range of notes in this section, which may appear quite daunting at first. There are also some high and low notes of the same name, their positions are shown on the fingerboard.

Remember to hold wrist loosely while striking the strings lightly in a steady rhythm of ↓ **down** and ↑ **up** strokes.

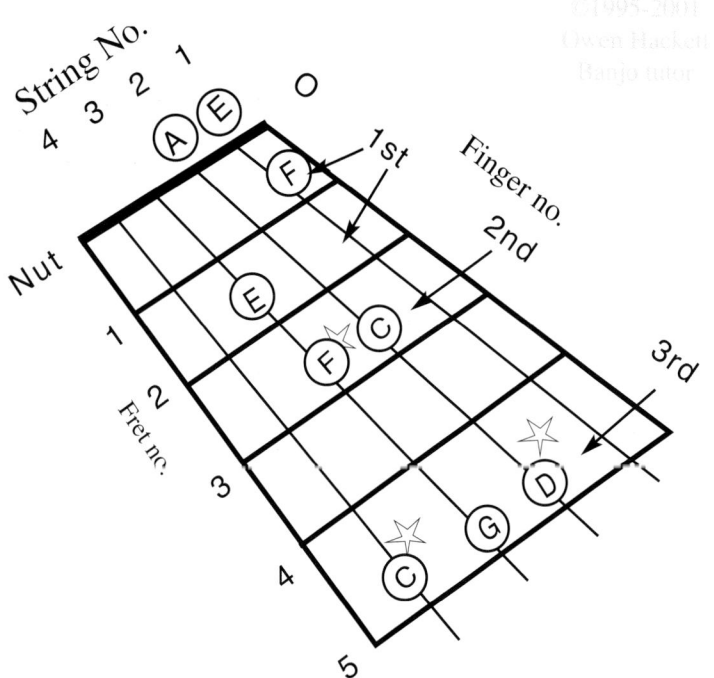

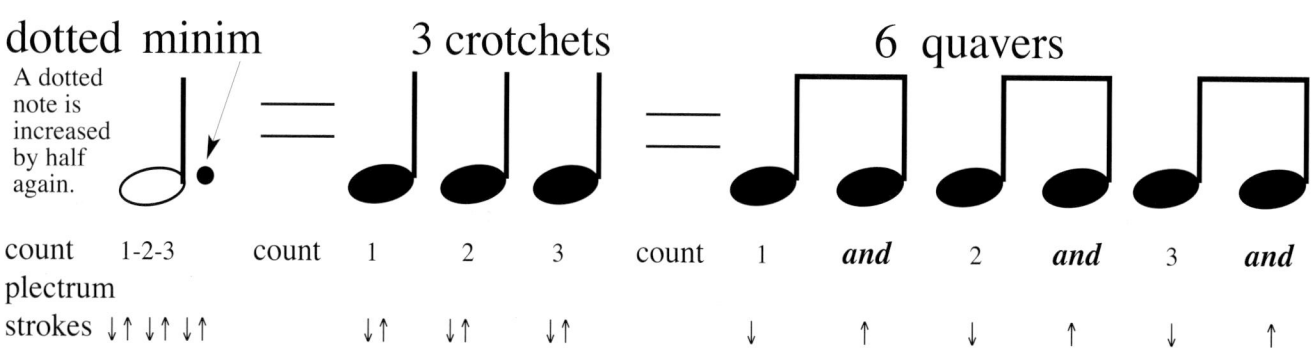

EXERCISE 6
PART 1

SPANCILL HILL in B min.

Ignore these two lead - in notes until you have mastered the rhythm

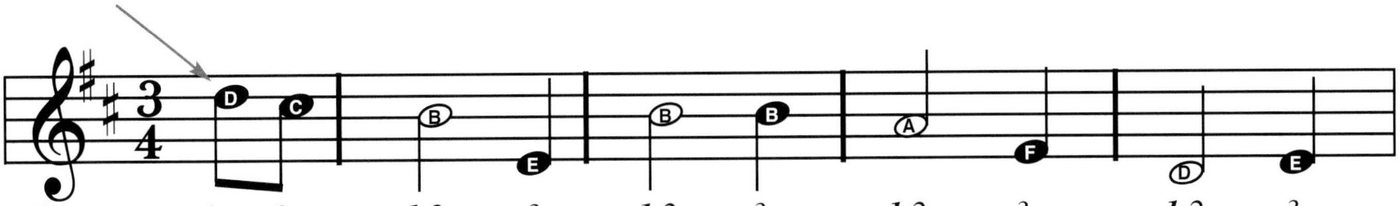

Here is a simplified version of Spancill Hill. Some players might use slightly different structure of notes, but for the moment what's here is fine. Try and stick to the plectrum guides given for this tune as they will improve your overall control of the plec'. The dot following the white half note (minim) gives it the new value of a 3/4 note. So instead of it getting ↓↑ ↓↑, (a count of 2); it now gets ↓↑ ↓↑ ↓↑ (a count of 3). The **tie** between the dotted **E** and the following **E** simply means that the first note only is sounded but held for it's own value *plus* the value of the note it is tied to. As this is not always practical on the banjo, the tied note may be played *without emphasis*.

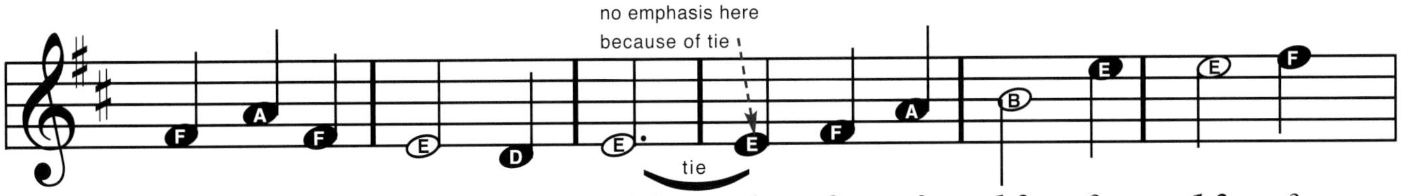

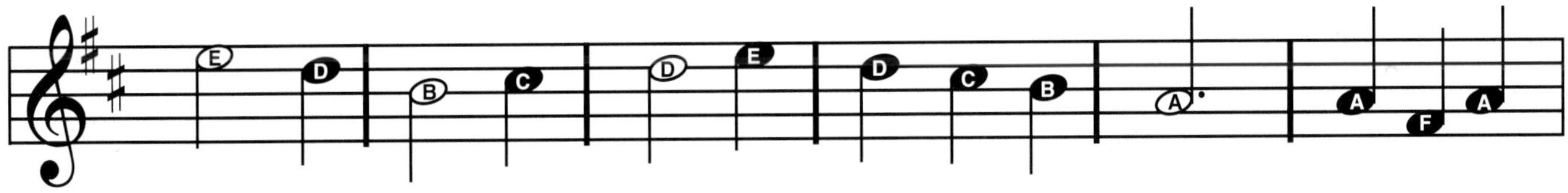

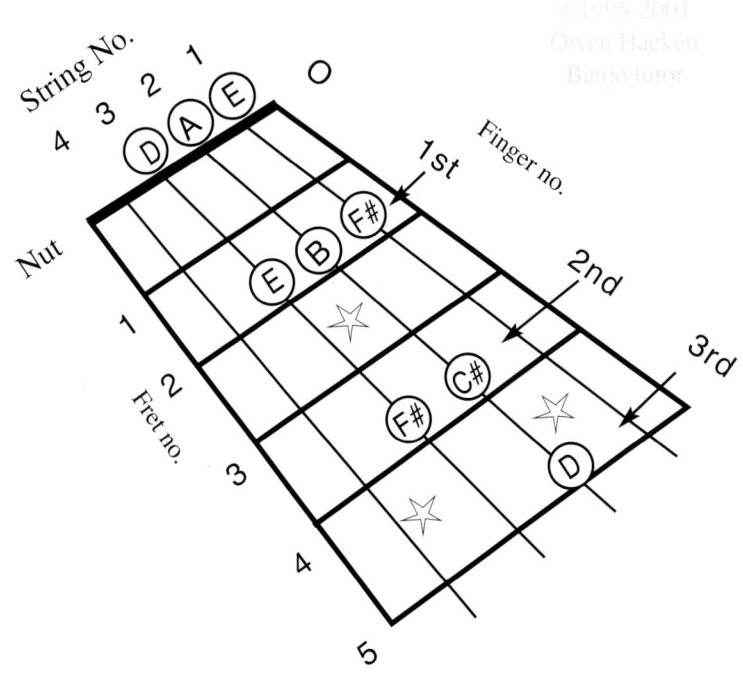

EXERCISE 6
PART 2

SPANCILL HILL in B min.

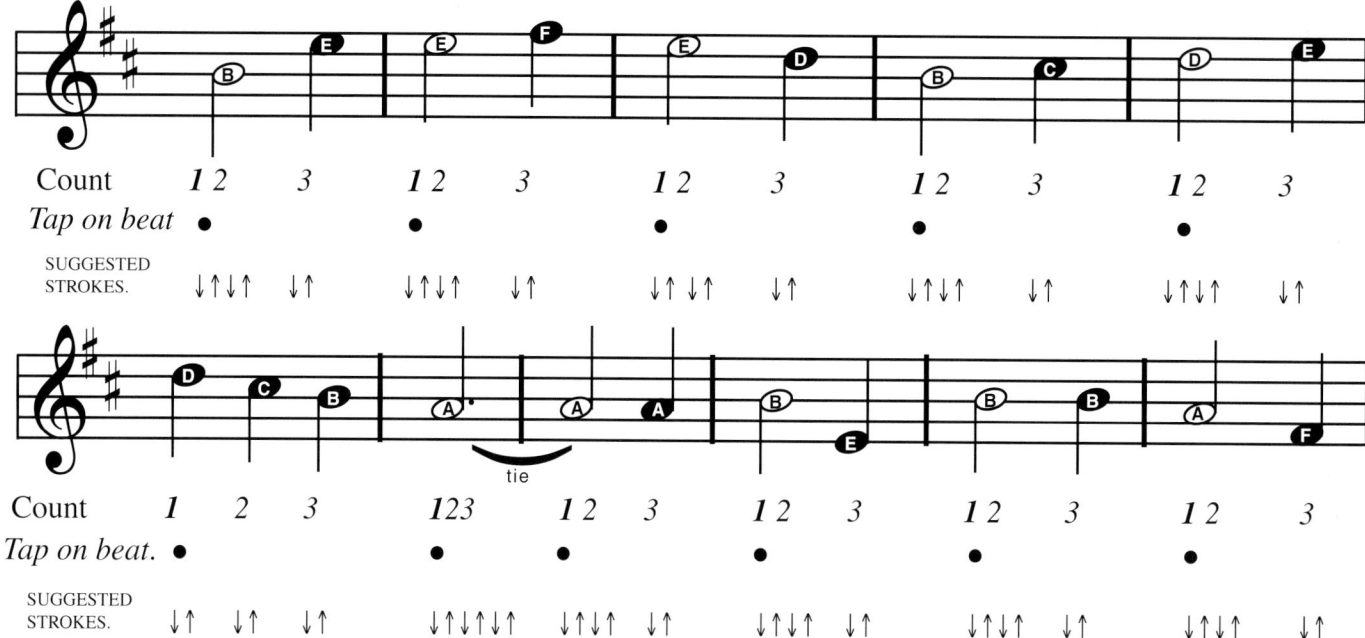

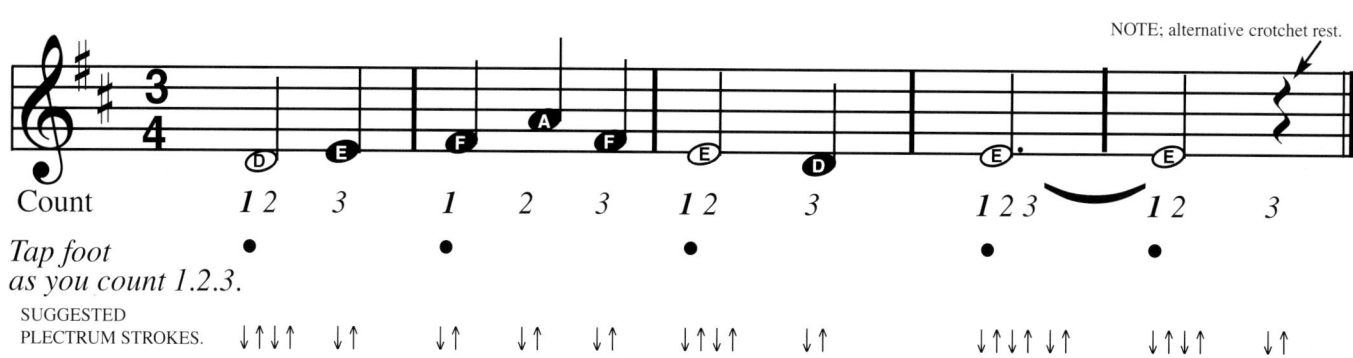

NOTE; alternative crotchet rest.

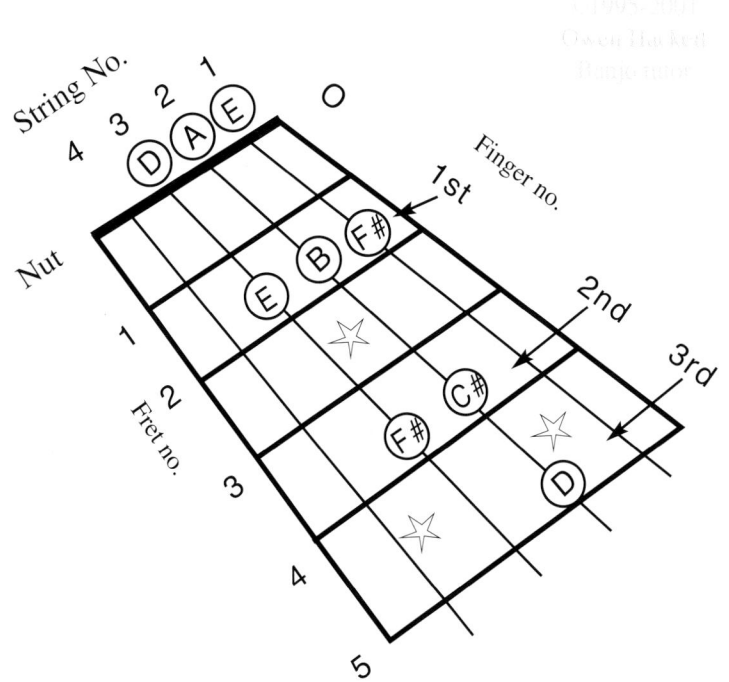

Please remember to hold the plectrum firmly but not too tightly; you will get a nicer tone from the strings if you allow it to *glide* over the strings; (let it slightly sway or swivel between thumb and finger.)

For the other hand, don't allow your thumb to hook over the fingerboard. Always keep unused fingers spread out ready for action over the fingerboard, close to the frets. Don't forget to tap your foot if you can, on the beat count (1).

Watch out for the sharp ♯ or flat ♭ signs at the beginning of the tune. Make a mental note of the notes to be sharpened or flattened.

Can you remember what key a tune is in, if it has a key signature of three sharps. What notes are sharpened?

Answer   A Maj or F♯ min.

EXERCISE 7

31

SHOE THE DONKEY. Mazurka in G

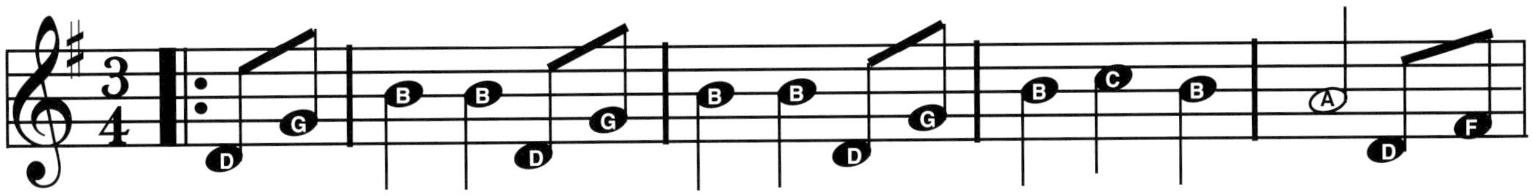

Count   3   &   1   2   3   &   1   2   3   &   1   2   3   1 2   3   &

Tap foot on beat
simplified
plectrum strokes   ↓   ↑   ↓   ↓   ↓   ↑   ↓   ↓   ↓   ↑   ↓   ↓   ↓   ↓ ↑   ↓   ↑

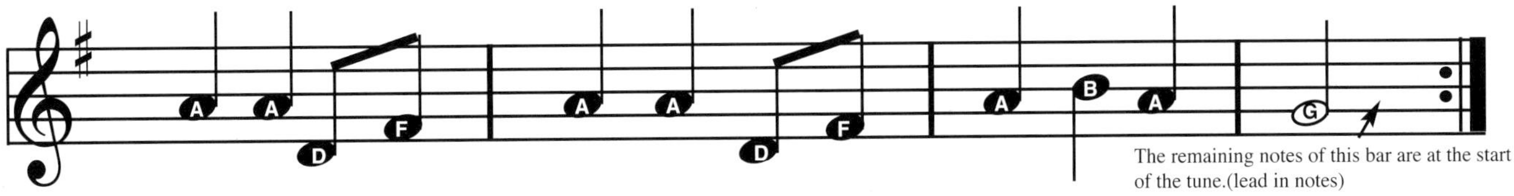

The remaining notes of this bar are at the start of the tune.(lead in notes)

Count   1   2   3   &   1   2   3   &   1   2   3   1 2

Tap foot on beat
plectrum strokes   ↓   ↓   ↓   ↑   ↓   ↓   ↓   ↑   ↓   ↓   ↓   ↓ ↑

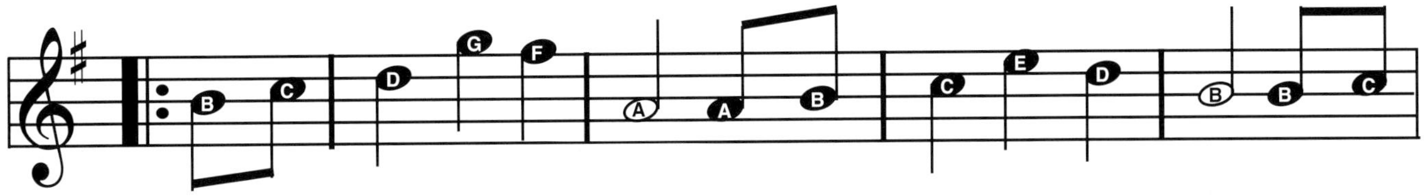

Count   3   &   1   2   3   1 2   3   &   1   2   3   1 2   3   &

Tap foot on beat

1st.   2nd.

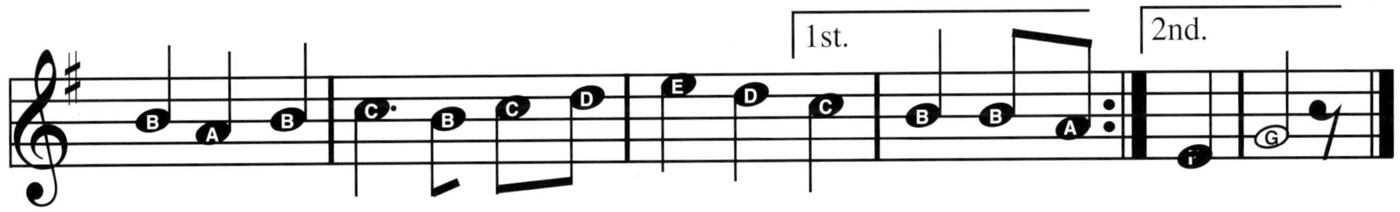

Count   1   2   3   1 2   &   3   &   1   2   3   1   2   &   3   1 2   3

Tap beat

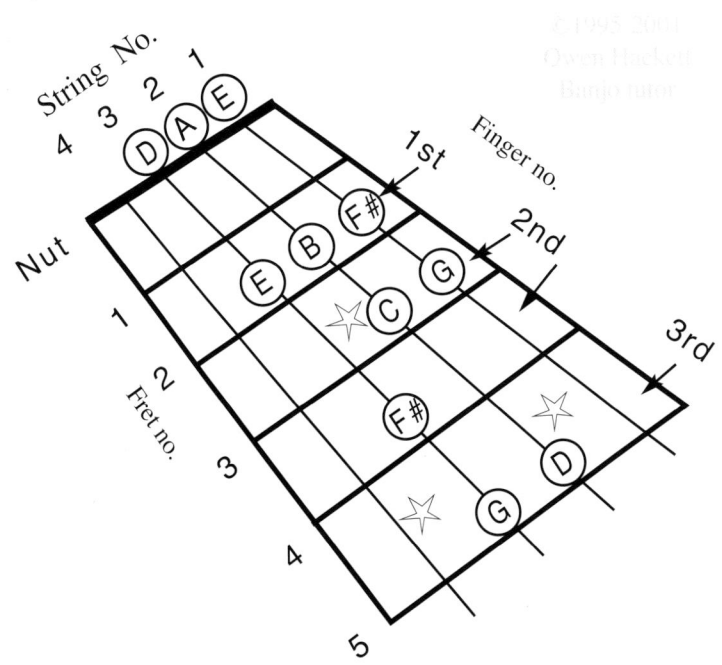

The way the last few bars of this tune are written, might present some difficulty for the beginner to understand. It was found in a ordinary music book so we decided to include it for your benefit. Look closely at the <u>3rd bar</u> of the last staff. Above the **C** is a 1st time sign. It means that from the **C** to the end of the next bar, you play the 1st time only. The 2nd time around when you get to this bar you play the **E** and **D** only, then you skip over the notes encompassed by the 1st time sign and play the **F** ending on the following long **G**. (Note the crotchet rest.)

32

EXERCISE 8

AN FHALAINGIN MHUIMHNEACH
Mazurka in G.

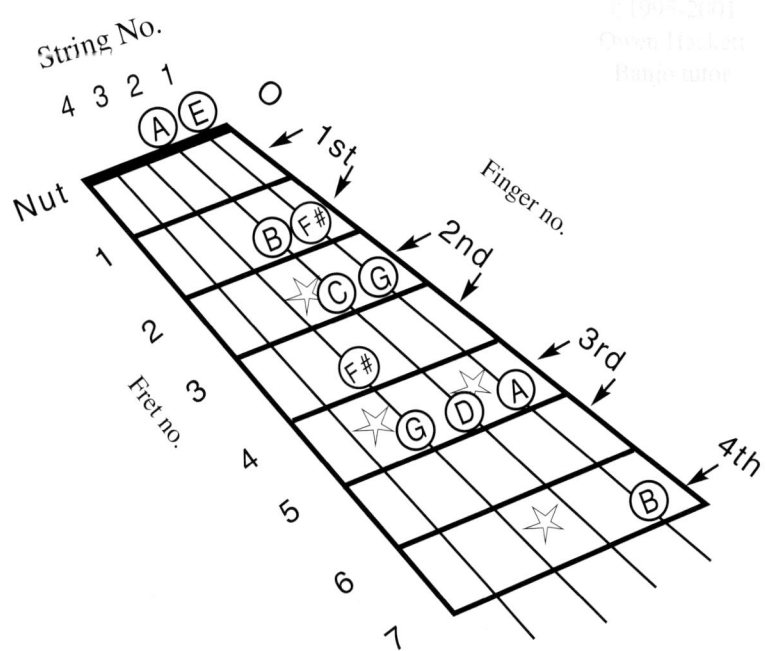

You will notice that in these 3/4 time waltz tunes, we have the beat sign • for the first note of each bar only (at the **1**). This helps the player achieve a nice swing to the tune. If you like however, you may tap your foot at the 2 and the 3 while learning and working out the beat / rhythm. Once you get the tune off properly, go back to the 1 tap per bar, as the 3 taps could lead to a hoppy mechanical rendition of the tune.

EXERCISE 9
PART 1

IDLE ROAD. Double Jig.

Try this exercise before beginning the tune below. Start by striking the **3rd** string (**D**) down ↓ on the count of **1**; continue down ↓ and strike the **2nd** string (**A**) on the count of **2**. On the way back up ↑, strike the **A** string again on the count of **3**. Continue up ↑ strike the **D** string again, for the count of **4**. Then back down ↓ to the **A** for **5** and back on the **A** for **6**. . Repeat the whole exercise a few times, being as accurate with the plectrum as you can, until you have mastered the rhythm of **1** 23, **4** 56. **1** 23, **4** 56.

This tune is a double jig, in **6/8** time. The rhythm is different to what we have learned so far. First practice counting aloud

1-2-3; **4**-5-6; **1**-2-3; **4**-5-6; etc.

Place *emphasis* on the **1** and a lesser emphasis on the **4**. Tap your foot on the **1** and **4**. What notes are sharp?

The above notes are quavers. (1/8th. notes) each receives one stroke of the plectrum. If, when you get to the note **C**, (a crotchet, 2nd bar) you find it difficult to get the counting & timing right, try **one** of the following methods;

1 strike it twice as if it were two quavers; or

2 make it a treble (see notes on *trebled*) or

3 when you count **4** simply rest the plectrum on the **E** string for count **5** then strike **E** for count **6**.

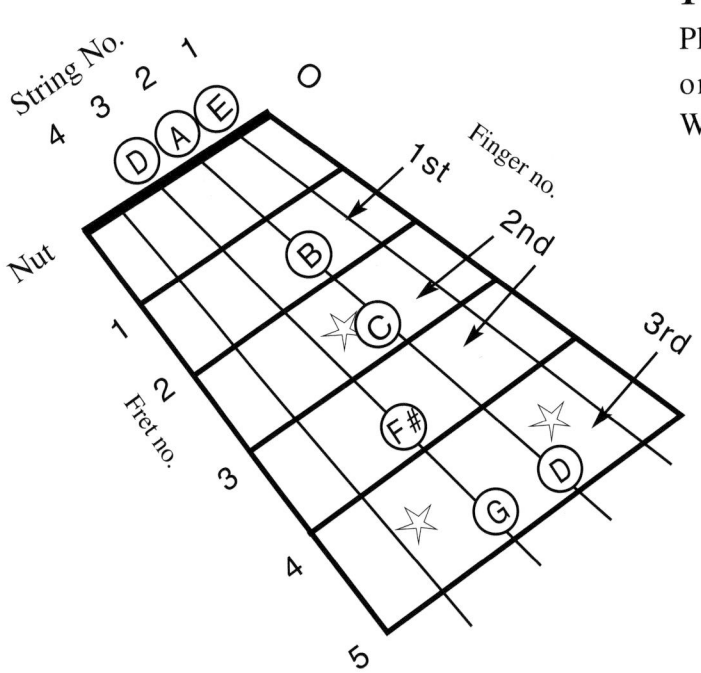

EXERCISE 9
PART 2

IDLE ROAD. Double Jig.

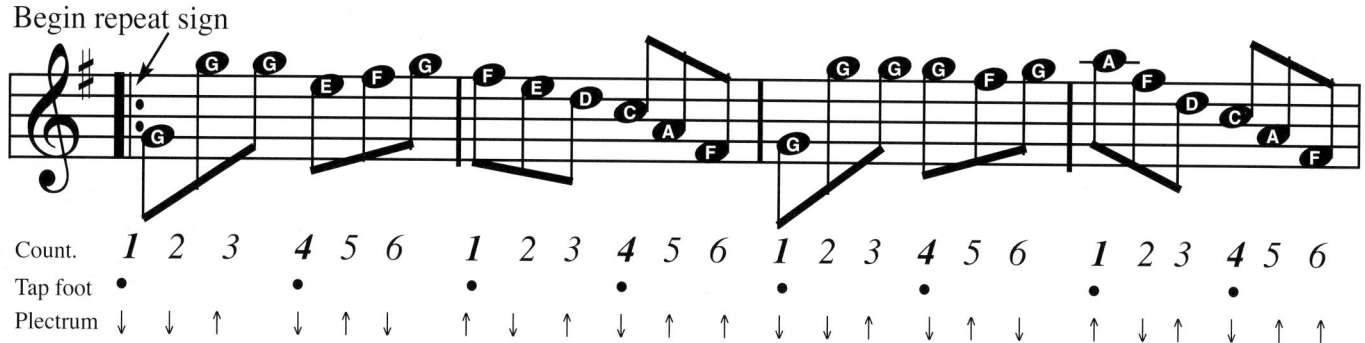

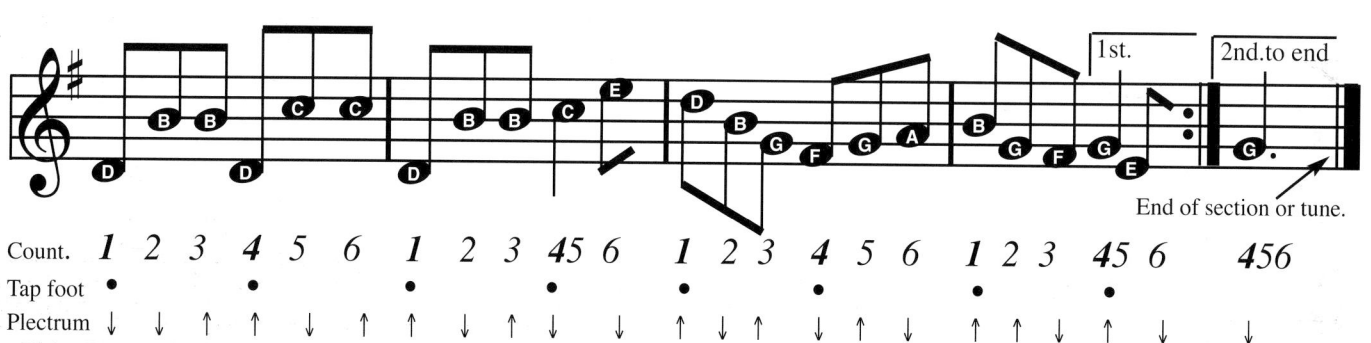

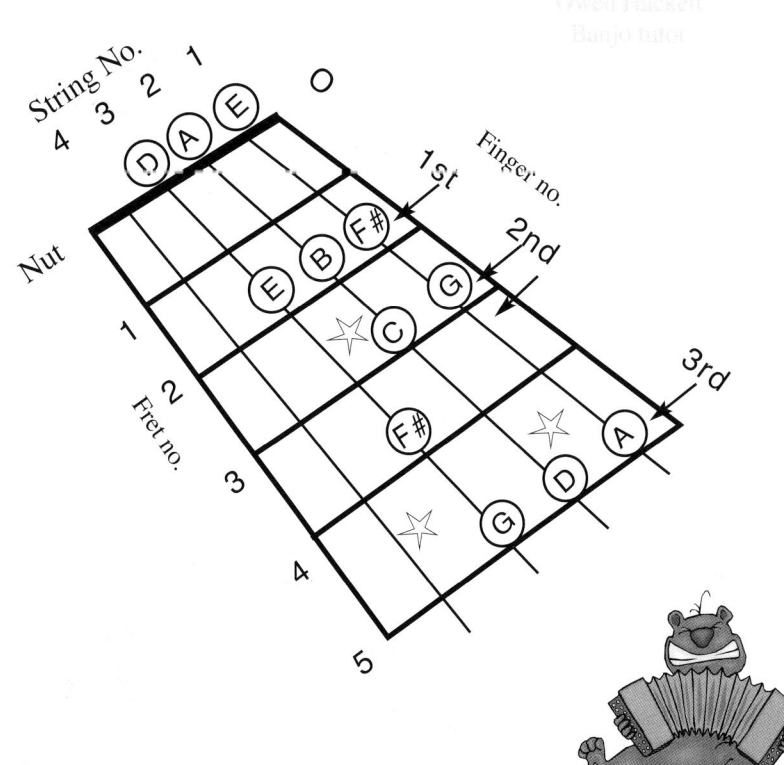

We'll be discontinuing with the plectrum guides after this page, (except where deemed necessary). If you have difficulty, just remember that you usually strike a string in the same direction that the plectrum was going, in order to get to that string. Otherwise use reciprocal (down ↓ and up ↑) strokes.

Practice counting and tapping out the rhythm before attempting any tune. This will give you an idea of how the rhythm of the tune should go.

EXERCISE 10

35

BRYAN O'LYNN. Double Jig in A minor.

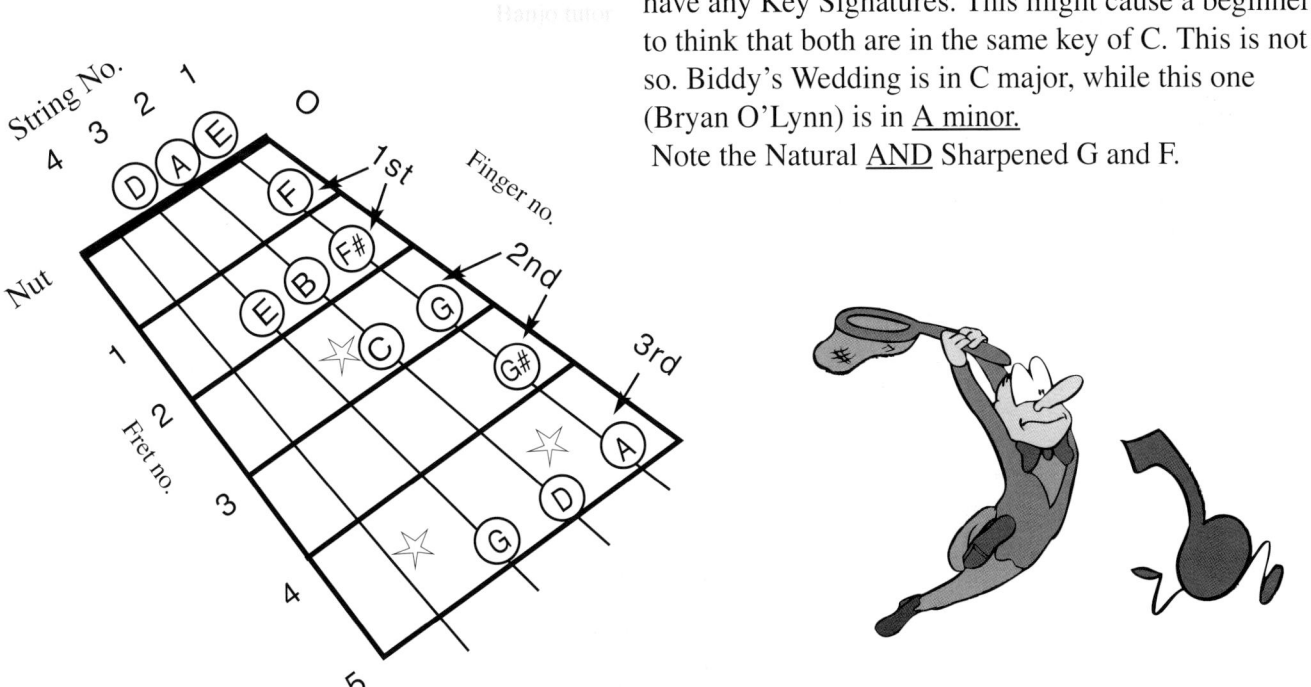

Neither this tune nor the next one, (Biddy's Wedding), have any Key Signatures. This might cause a beginner to think that both are in the same key of C. This is not so. Biddy's Wedding is in C major, while this one (Bryan O'Lynn) is in A minor.

Note the Natural AND Sharpened G and F.

EXERCISE 11

BIDDY'S WEDDING. Double Jig in C

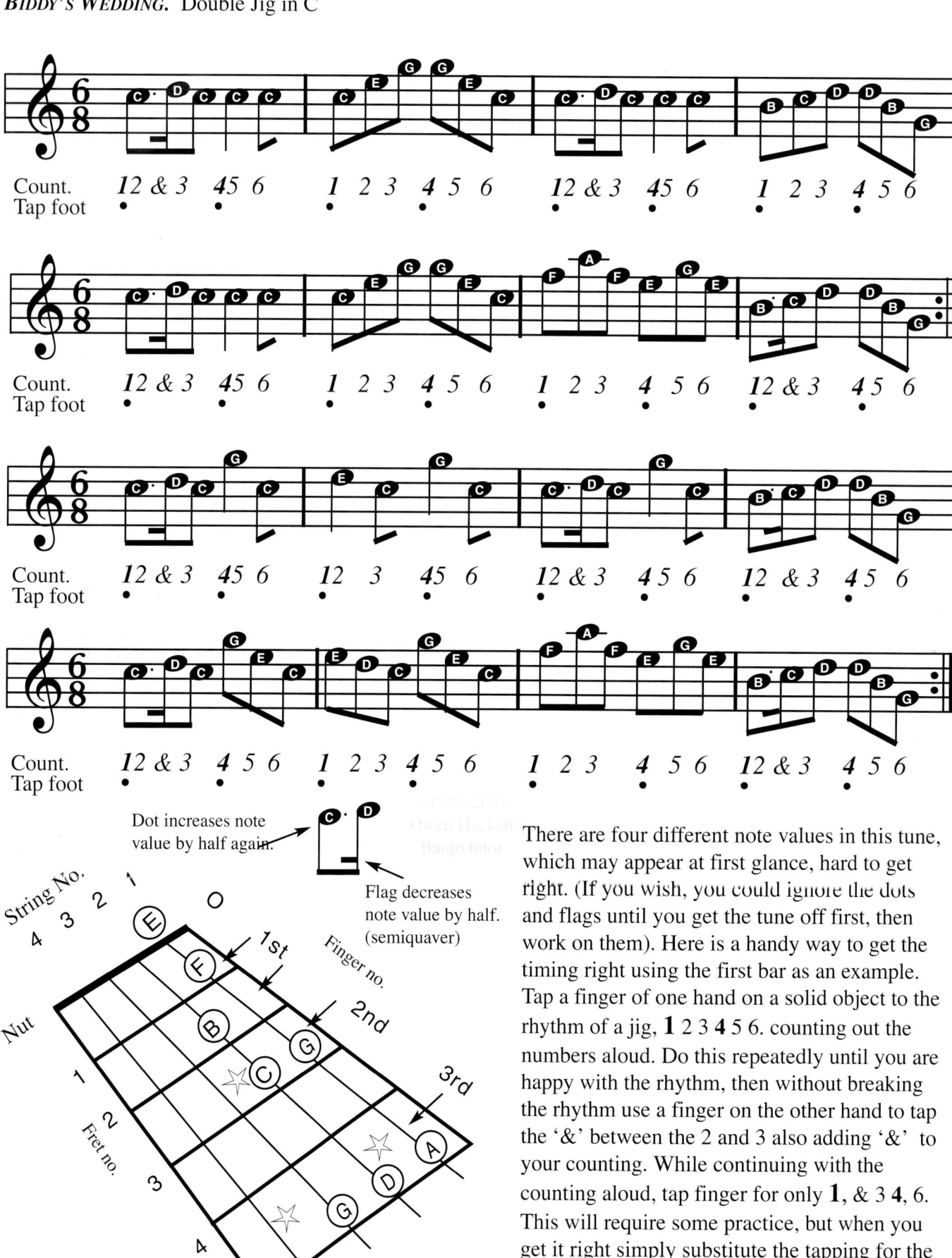

There are four different note values in this tune, which may appear at first glance, hard to get right. (If you wish, you could ignore the dots and flags until you get the tune off first, then work on them). Here is a handy way to get the timing right using the first bar as an example. Tap a finger of one hand on a solid object to the rhythm of a jig, **1** 2 3 **4** 5 6. counting out the numbers aloud. Do this repeatedly until you are happy with the rhythm, then without breaking the rhythm use a finger on the other hand to tap the '&' between the 2 and 3 also adding '&' to your counting. While continuing with the counting aloud, tap finger for only **1**, & 3 **4**, 6. This will require some practice, but when you get it right simply substitute the tapping for the notes.

EXERCISE 12

37

PADDY'S RETURN. Double Jig

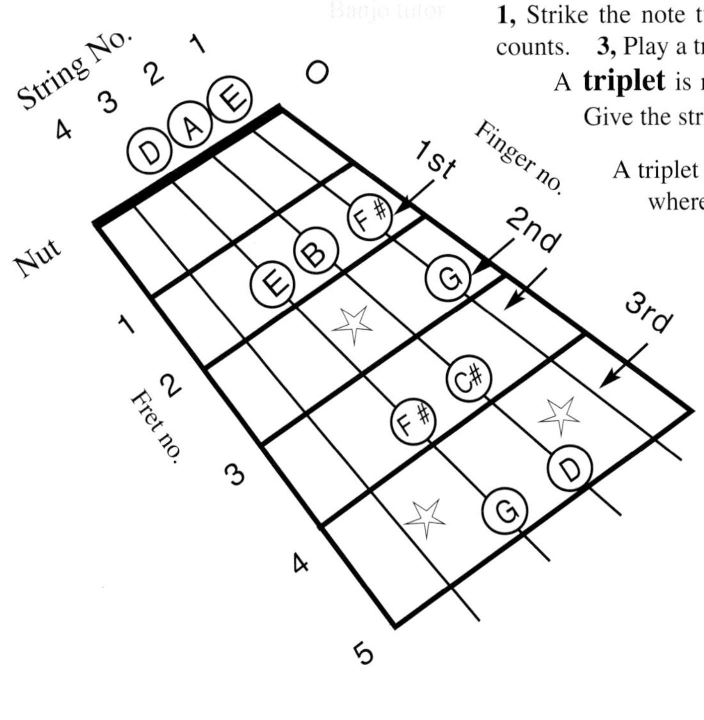

Remember, you can play the crotchets any of three ways as described earlier.
1, Strike the note twice as if it were two quavers.   **2,** Hold the note for two counts.   **3,** Play a triplet or (treble.)

A **triplet** is really three notes in the time of two, (Quavers in this tune). Give the string 3 quick CONTROLLED ↓↑↓ flicks of the plectrum.

A triplet can be written as a crotchet where the three notes are the same.

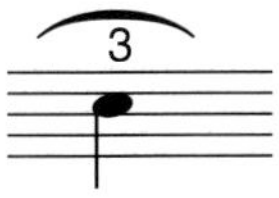

If the three notes are different, then they might be written like this;

These notes can be any combination, and the triplet sign can be below or above the staff. Playing them is more demanding, as the the different notes have to be plectrummed and fingered simultaneously. To help get the rhythm of a triplet right, try saying
-DID-IL- Y- playing the notes at the same time. Try tripling some crotchets above. Some players tend to play the triplets faster than the rest of the tune demands, and spoil the timing of the tune. Take extra care to keep triplets flowing **with** the rest of the tune.

EXERCISE 13

THE ABSENT MINDED MAN. Double Jig.

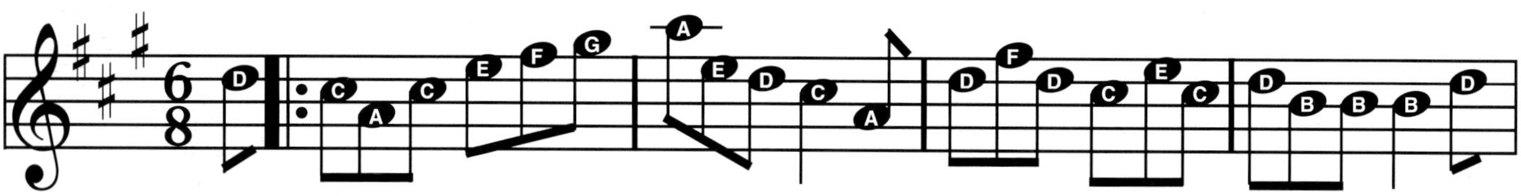

[Musical notation with notes labeled]

Line 1: D | C A C E F G | A E D C A | D D D C C | D B B B B D
Count: 6 | 1 2 3 4 5 6 | 1 2 3 45 6 | 1 2 3 4 5 6 | 1 2 3 45 6

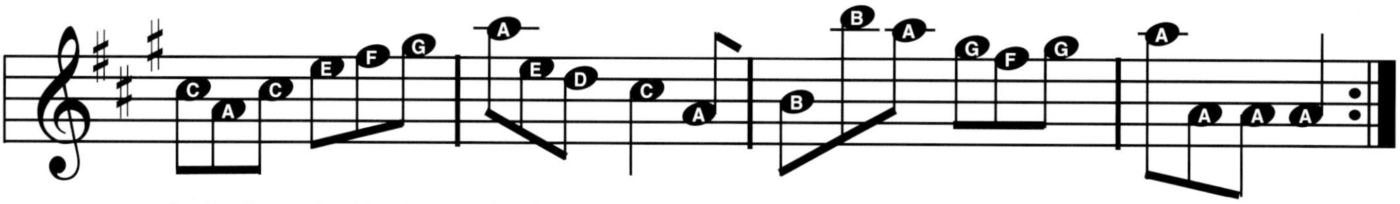

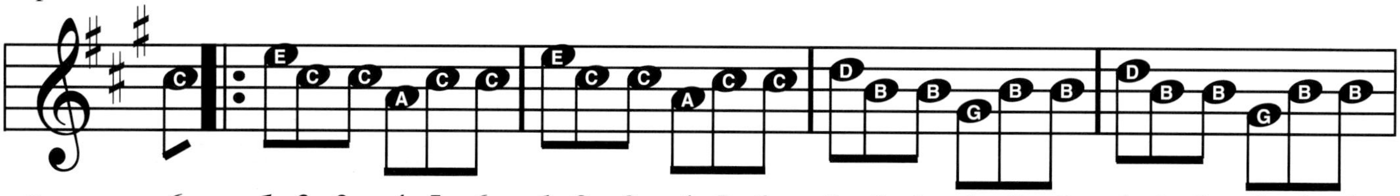

Line 2: C A C E F G | A E D C | B A G F G | A A A
Count: 1 2 3 4 5 6 | 1 2 3 45 6 | 1 2 3 4 5 6 | 1 2 3 45

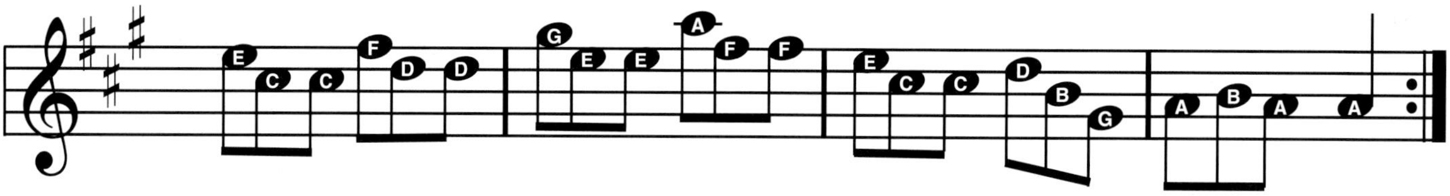

Line 3: C | E C A C E C A C | E C A C D B G B | D B B B B B
Count: 6 | 1 2 3 4 5 6 | 1 2 3 4 5 6 | 1 2 3 4 5 6 | 1 2 3 4 5 6

Line 4: E C C F D D | E E E G A F F | E C C D B | G A B A A
Count: 1 2 3 4 5 6 | 1 2 3 4 5 6 | 1 2 3 4 5 6 | 1 2 3 45

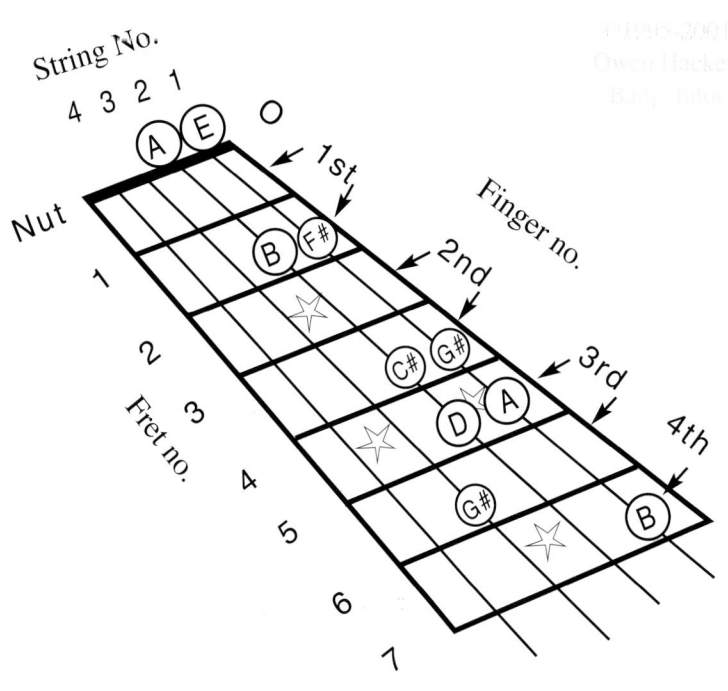

Do you know what key this tune is in? The three sharps are C.F.G. That means all these notes in this tune are sharpened, raised one semitone (one fret.) The only new notes are G♯ and high B. fingering the high B, can present a problem for beginners, but it is good for stretching the fingers. Allow the thumb to act as a swivel point for the rest of the fingers and swing around on it, stretching the little finger (4th,) to land accurately just behind the 7th. fret. Then simply walk fingers back along the A, G and F notes with 3rd, 2nd and 1st fingers, repositioning your hand for continued playing.

EXERCISE 13
PART 2

The Absent Minded Man. Double jig.

Note position of thumb, and finger just behind seventh fret.

Did you notice anything unusual about the last bar (the one with the end repeat sign), on both the 2nd and last line of music? (Previous page). Well, if you count the notes, you'll find one to the value of a quaver missing. A good many music books are written like this. When you get to the **end repeat** sign in these cases, you simply go back to the **beginning**, or until you encounter a **begin repeat** sign then play the lead-in note(s) again. When you get to the very ending of the tune, just allow the tune to end as if it had a dot or rest to the value of the missing note(s), after the final written note.

1

Let's put some ornamentation into this tune. Starting on the 1st. bar of The Absent Minded Man, (the C♯, A, C♯).

2

Take the first two notes C♯ A and play a triplet by adding a B between them.

3

As mentioned earlier, a triplet is played in the same time as **TWO** notes. We now have to insert another note to make up the time difference.

We'll use the C♯ because it is the last note of the three we altered, also it's the note leading up the the next three notes in the bar. The rhythm of the triplet plus the following quaver should go like the rhythm of these words; (Did-i-ly dum).

4

The music could also be written like this, **Without** any treble sign.

5

A note as written below, (C♯ with a dot, in the example;) may also be played as a triplet (plus a note for the dot).

EXERCISE 14

O'Gallagher's Frolics. in D minor

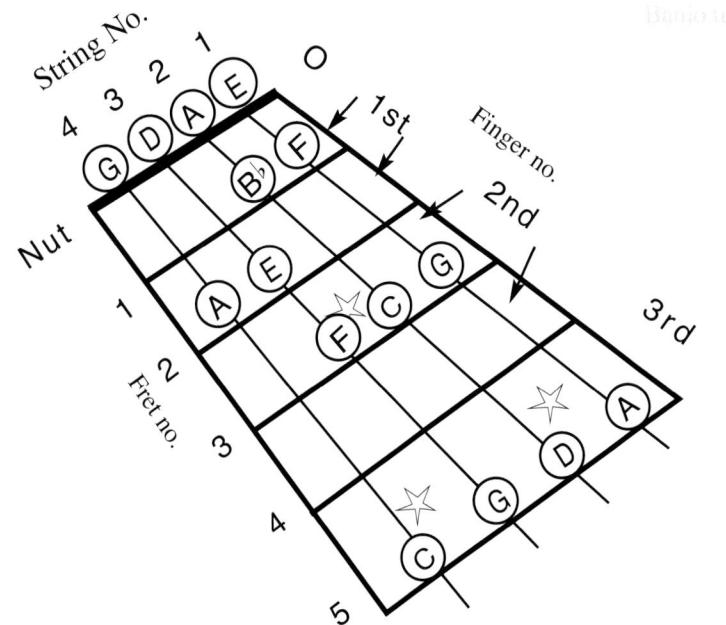

This tune is in the key of D Minor. It has one flattened note, B.
Try this tune without the aid of the beat or counting guides.

EXERCISE 15
PART 1

41

Drops OF Brandy. In G.
Slip or Hop Jig (1st Half)

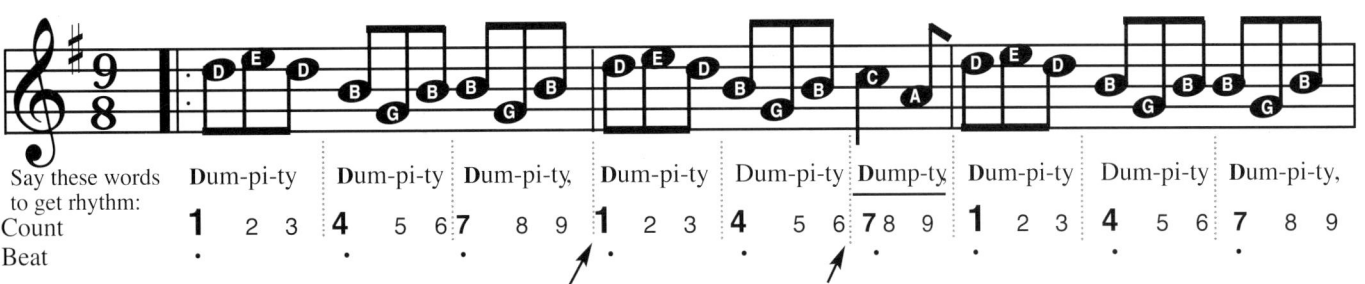

Say these words to get rhythm: Dum-pi-ty Dum-pi-ty Dum-pi-ty Dum-pi-ty Dum-pi-ty Dump-ty Dum-pi-ty Dum-pi-ty Dum-pi-ty,

Count Beat 1 2 3 4 5 6 7 8 9 1 2 3 4 5 6 7 8 9 1 2 3 4 5 6 7 8 9

Please note, that these little faint lines are inserted only to show where divisions are, where the notes and instructions are close together.

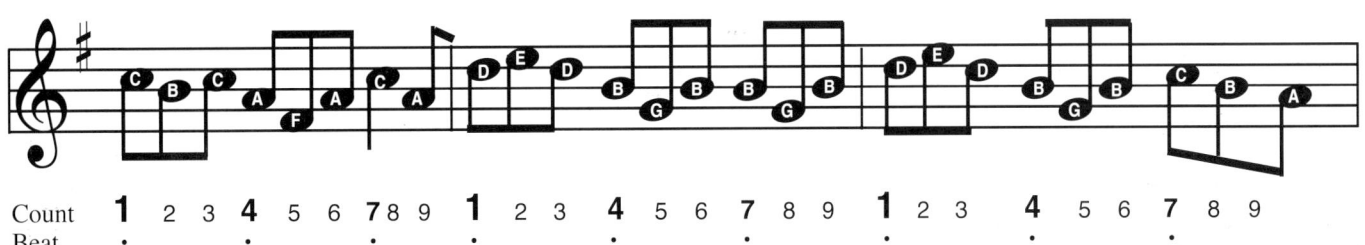

Count Beat 1 2 3 4 5 6 7 8 9 1 2 3 4 5 6 7 8 9 1 2 3 4 5 6 7 8 9

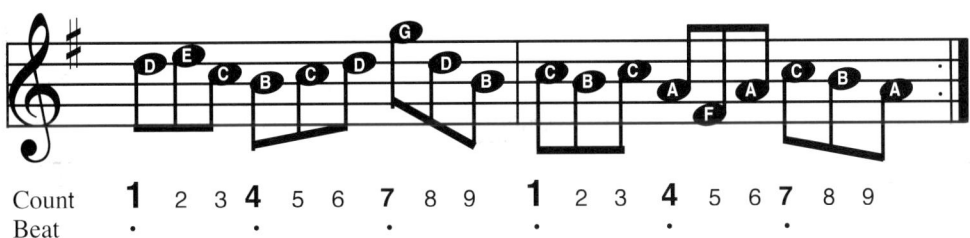

Count Beat 1 2 3 4 5 6 7 8 9 1 2 3 4 5 6 7 8 9

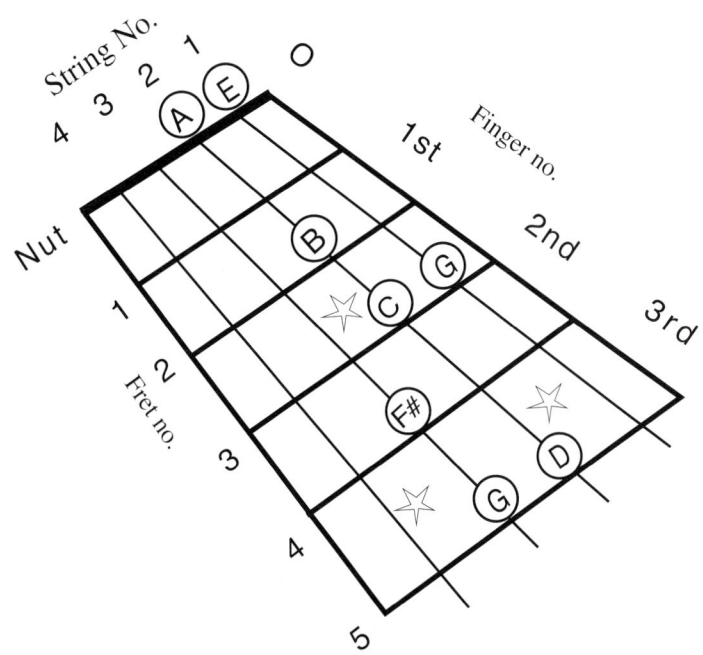

In this slip jig, there are 9 quavers ($1/8$ notes) per bar. It is not necessary to actually count to 9 as you play; 1-2-3. 1-2-3. 1-2-3. is fine as long as you remember that there are three beats in each bar, not two like in the double jigs. Before attempting to play the tune, count out the rhythm while tapping your foot on each beat.

When you feel you have the rhythm right pick out the notes for the first bar only; get that bar right before going on to the next bar. Then get the second bar right. When you have it right, add the first bar and play the two bars. Then learn the third bar, add the first two, play the three bars, and so on. Doing it this way makes it easier for you to learn the tune quickly and accurately.

42

EXERCISE 15
PART 2

Drops Of Brandy. in G. (2nd Half)
Slip or Hop Jig

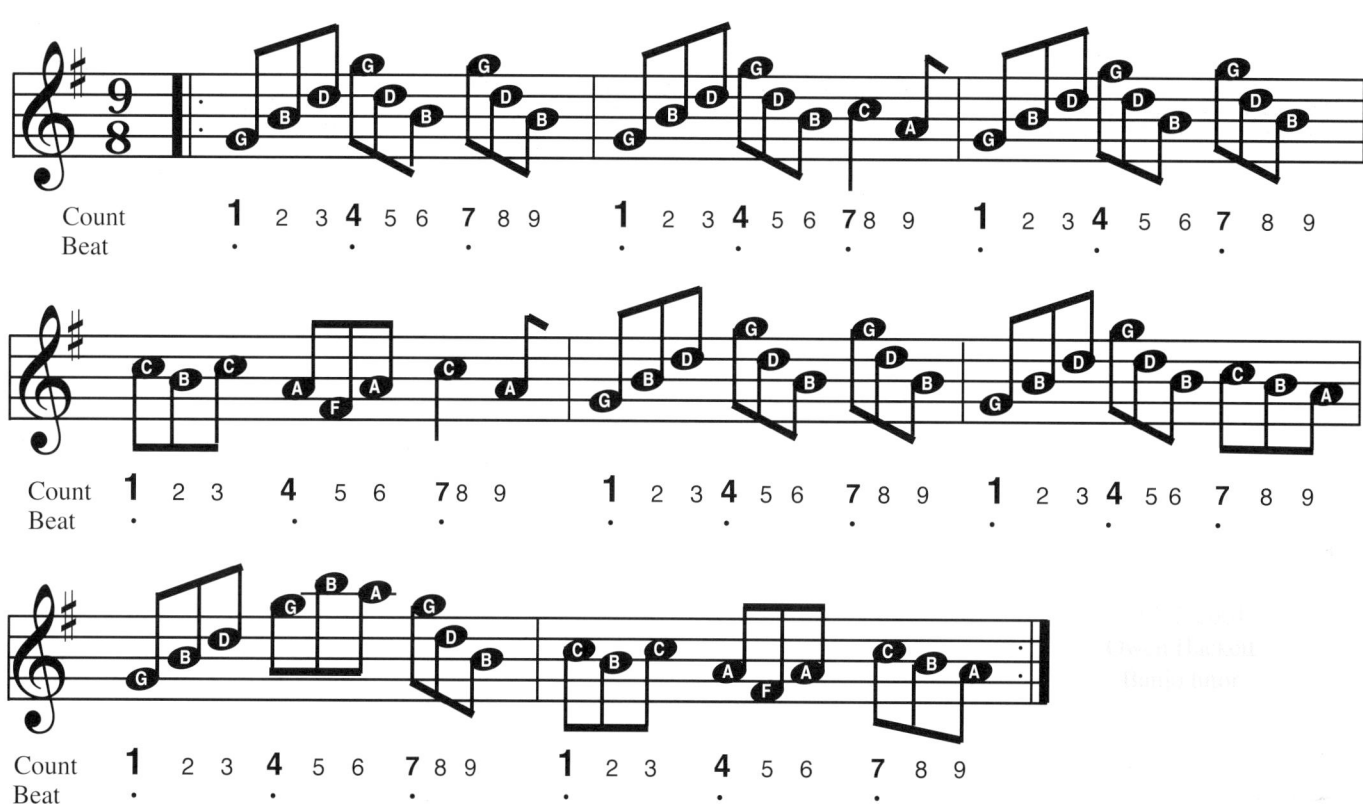

Tip:
In order to help you learn the names of the notes off by heart, you might like to try moving the book further away from you so the note names written within the note becomes less distinct, therefore encouraging you to memorise the note name.

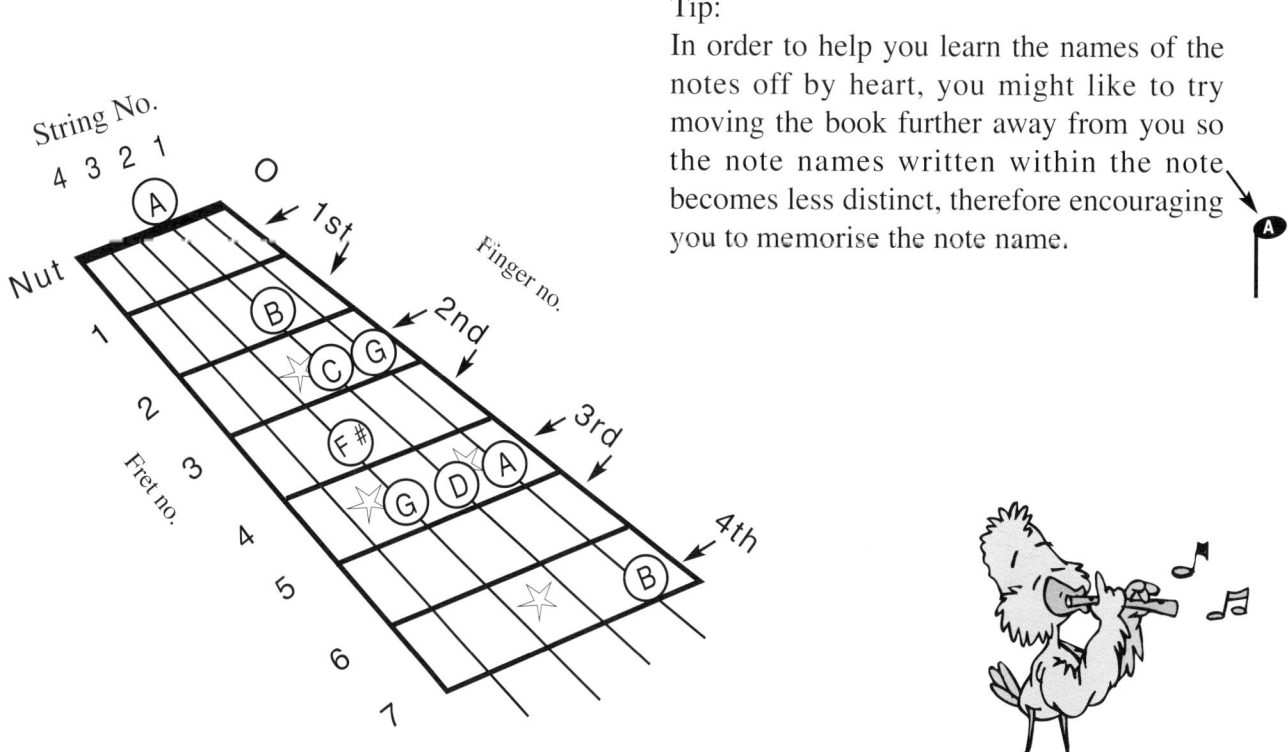

EXERCISE 16
PART 1

I Have A Wife Of My Own. In G.
Slip or Hop Jig   (1st Half)

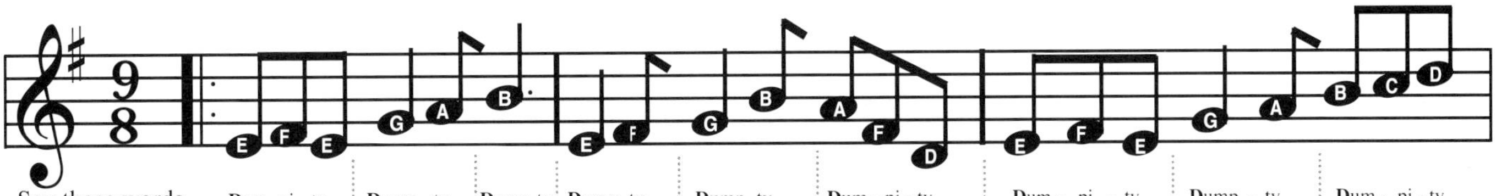

[Musical notation - first line with notes E F E G A B, E F G A F D, E F E G A B C D]

Say these words to get rhythm:
Count Beat

Dum-pi-ty Dump-ty Dump-ty Dump-ty Dump-ty Dum-pi-ty Dum-pi-ty Dump-ty Dum-pi-ty
1 2 3   4 5 6   7 8 9   1 2 3   4 5 6   7 8 9   1 2 3   4 5 6   7 8 9

| 3 quavers = 3 strokes Count of 3. | 1 Crotchet = 1 stroke Count of 2. | 1 Quaver = 1 stroke Count of 1 | Dotted crotchet =1 stroke; count of 3. **or** 3 strokes; count of 3. (Try alternate style) |

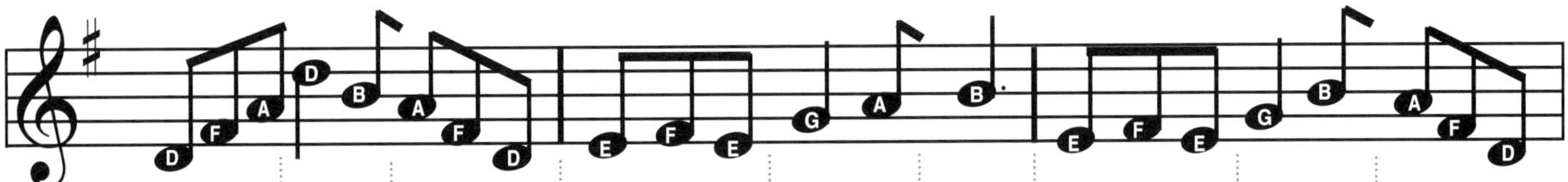

[Musical notation - second line]

Dum-pi-ty Dump-ty Dum-pi-ty Dum-pi-ty Dump-ty Dump-ty Dum-pi-ty Dump-ty Dum-pi-ty

Count Beat
1 2 3   4 5 6   7 8 9   1 2 3   4 5 6   7 8 9   1 2 3   4 5 6   7 8 9

[Musical notation - third line]

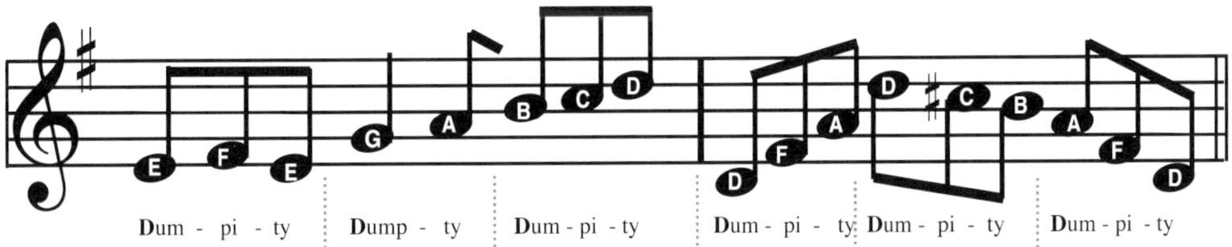

Dum-pi-ty Dump-ty Dum-pi-ty Dum-pi-ty Dum-pi-ty Dum-pi-ty

Count Beat
1 2 3   4 5 6   7 8 9   1 2 3   4 5 6   7 8 9

This slip jig is also in the key of G, but it has an accidental C♯. Not all the C's are sharpened - only the ones in the 8th, 12th and 16th bars. The note structure is also different; in bar 1, you have three quavers, then a crotchet, followed by a quaver and a dotted crotchet B. This B can either be held or played as three B notes, similar to three quavers.

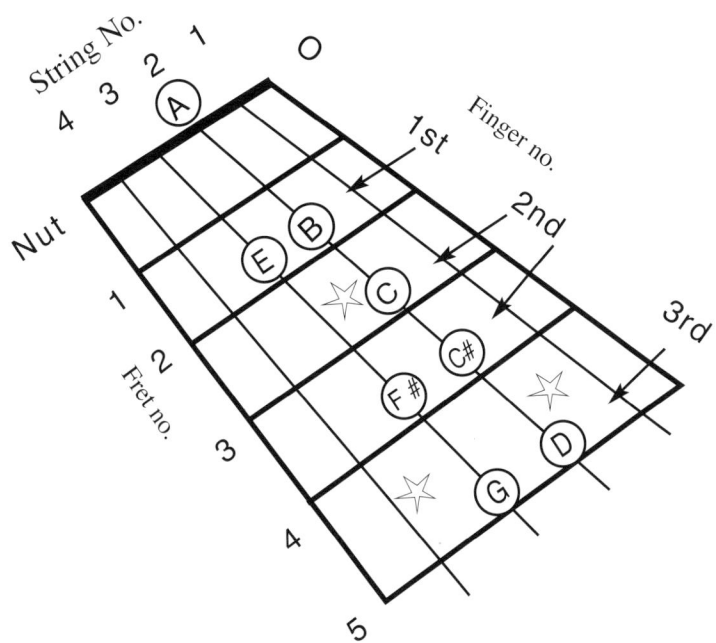

EXERCISE 16
PART 2

I Have A Wife Of My Own. In G.
(2nd Half)

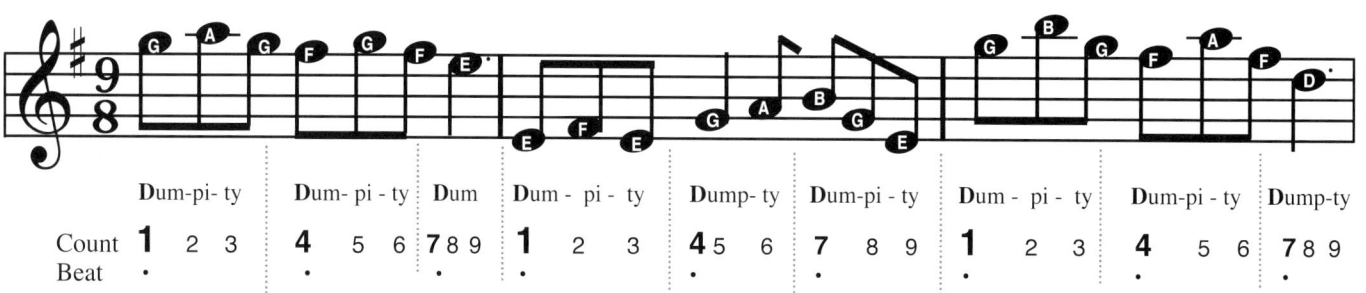

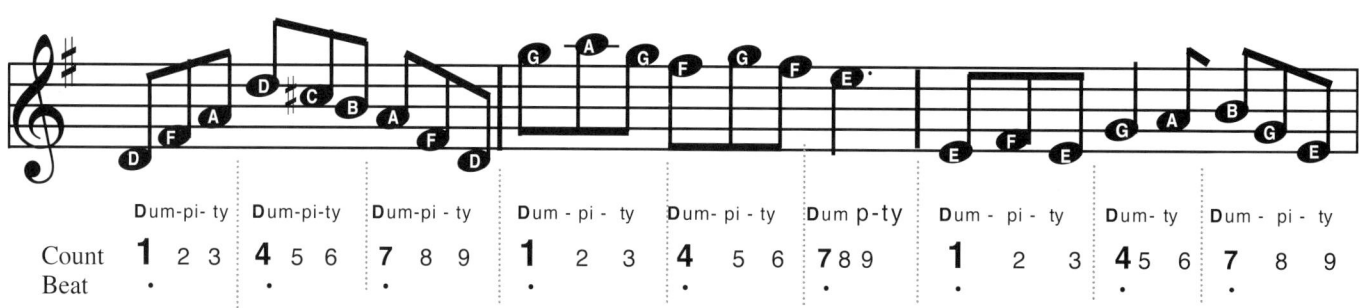

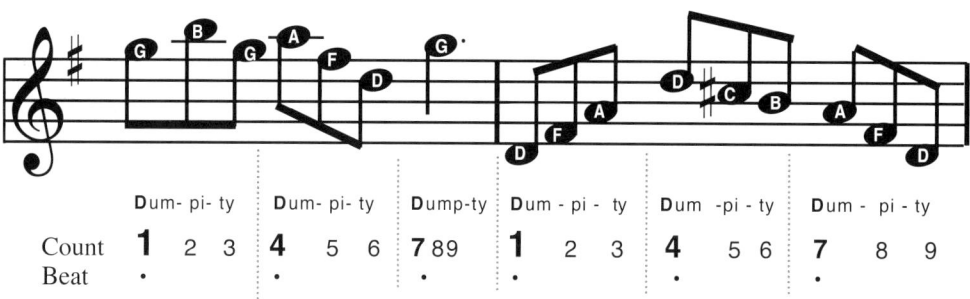

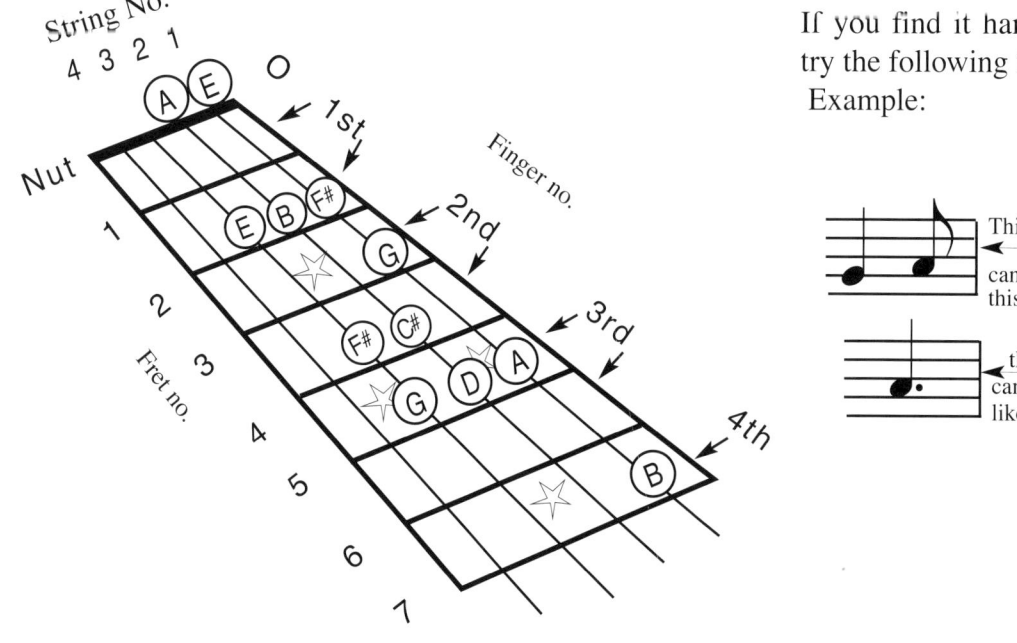

If you find it hard to get the timing right, try the following for starters.
 Example:

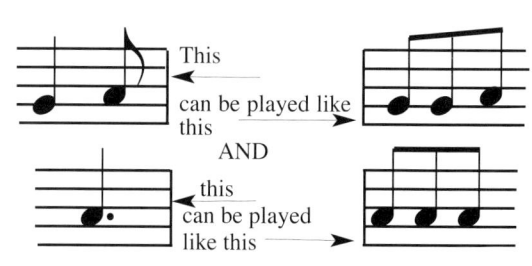

EXERCISE 17

45

Hunting The Hare. In D (2 sharps)
Slip or Hop Jig

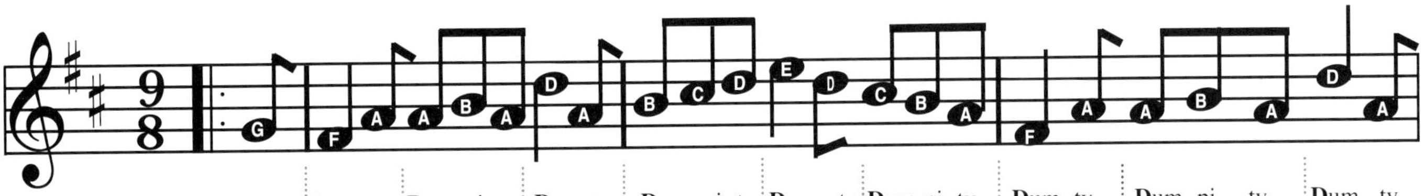

Say these words to get rhythm: -ty | Dum-ty | Dum-pi-ty | Dum-ty | Dum-pi-ty | Dum-ty | Dum-pi-ty | Dum-ty | Dum-pi-ty | Dum-ty

Count: 9 | 1 2 3 | 4 5 6 | 7 8 9 | 1 2 3 | 4 5 6 | 7 8 9 | 1 2 3 | 4 5 6 | 7 8 9

Beat

| 3 quavers = 3 strokes Count of 3. | 1 Crotchet = 1 stroke Count of 2. | 1 Quaver = 1 stroke Count of 1 | Dotted crotchet =1 stroke; count of 3. **or** 3 strokes; count of 3. (Try to alternate style) |

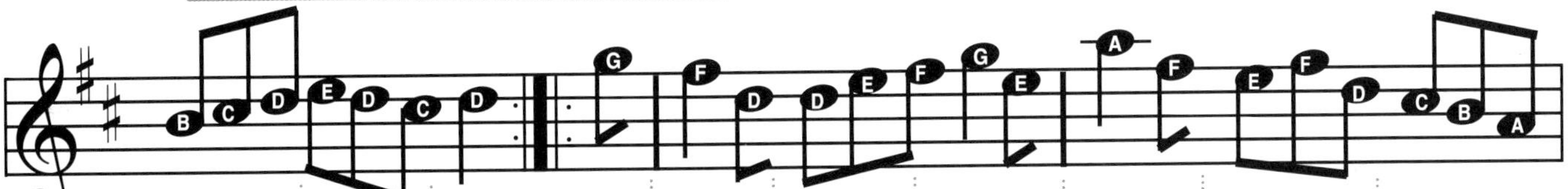

Dum-pi-ty | Dum-pi-ty | Dum | -ty | Dum-ty | Dum-pi-ty | Dum-ty | Dum-ty | Dum-pi-ty | Dum-pi-ty

Count: 1 2 3 | 4 5 6 | 7 8 | 9 | 1 2 3 | 4 5 6 | 7 8 9 | 1 2 3 | 4 5 6 | 7 8 9

Beat

These little lines are only to help you align the counting - beats - etc. with the right notes.

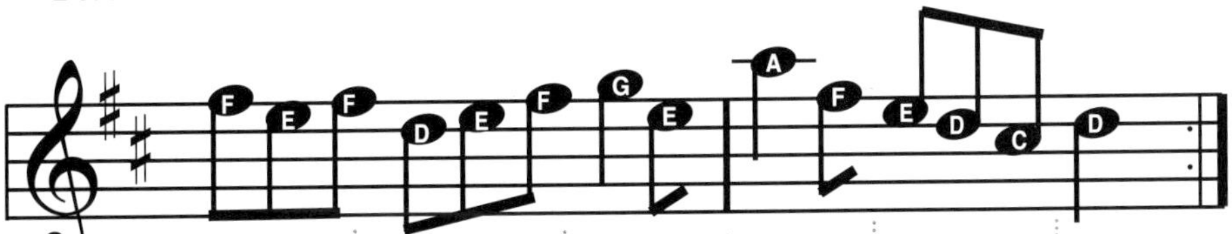

Dum-pi-ty | Dum-pi-ty | Dum-ty | Dum-ty | Dum-pi-ty | Dum

Count: 1 2 3 | 4 5 6 | 7 8 9 | 1 2 3 | 4 5 6 | 7 8

Beat

This tune has repeat signs at the beginning, middle and end. If in doubt what to do, refer back to page 23. Also you'll notice that there is one quaver missing in the last bar of each section. Can you remember why? and what to do? If not, turn to The Absent Minded Man page 38.

Remember not to hold the plectrum too tightly, and swivel the thumb on the fingerboard.

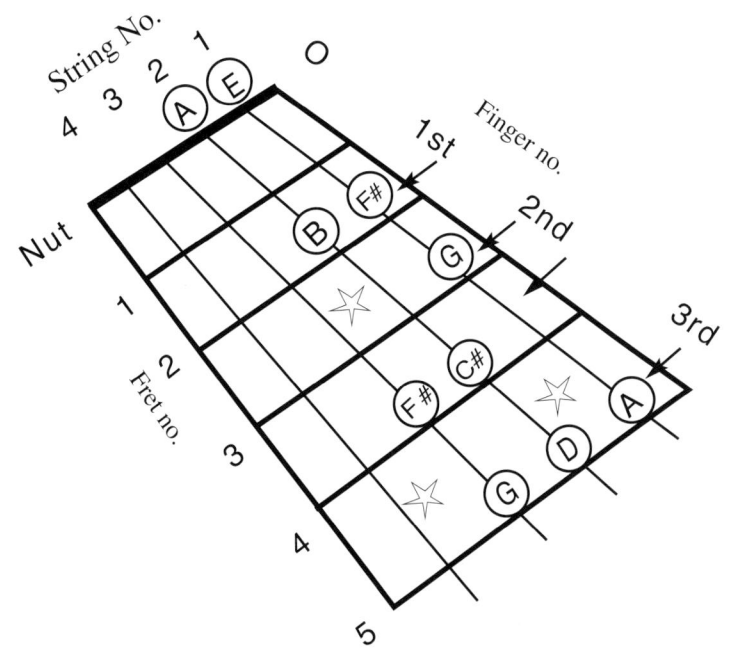

EXERCISE 18

Dever The Dancer. In B min. (2 sharps)
Slip or Hop Jig

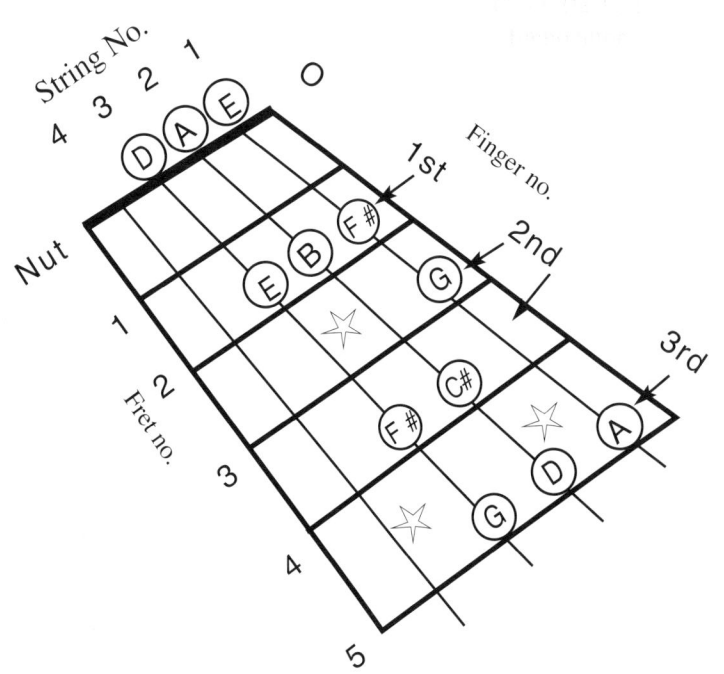

At first glance, one might think this tune was in D the same key as the previous one. Each Major key has a relative minor key. The relative minor of D maj. is B min. See Scales at beginning of tutor.

EXERCISE 19
PARTS 1 & 2

Barney Brallaghan. In D Maj. (2 sharps)
3 part Slip or Hop Jig. Parts 1 & 2 on this page

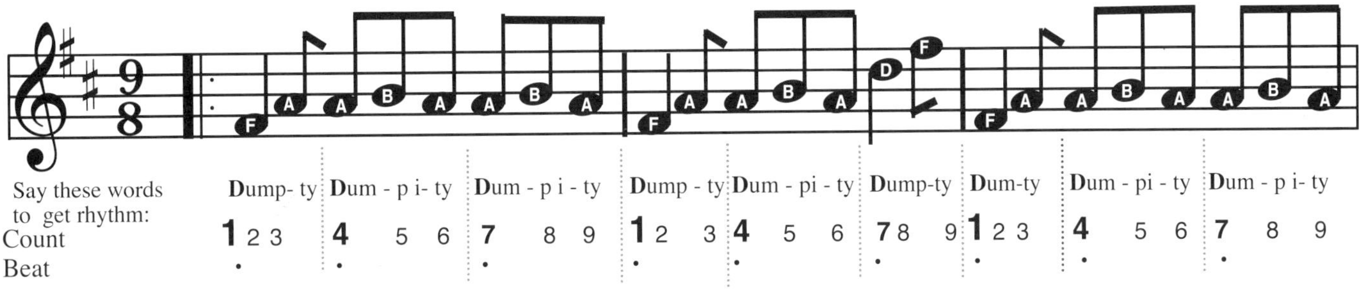

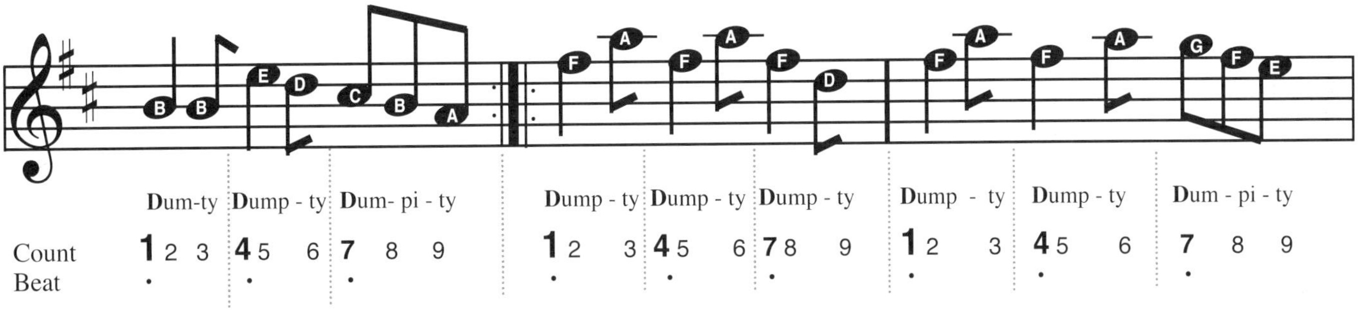

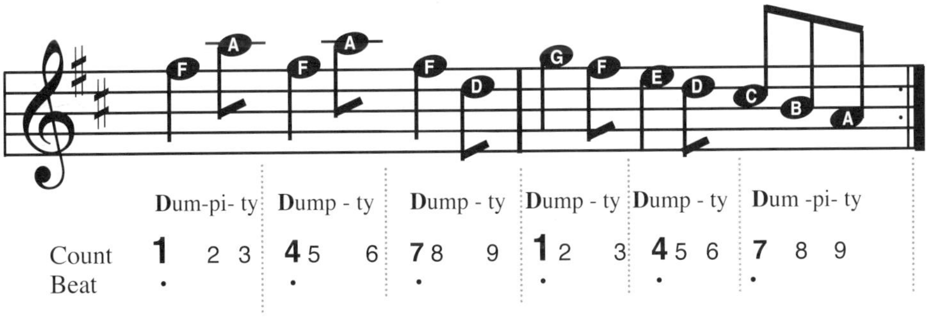

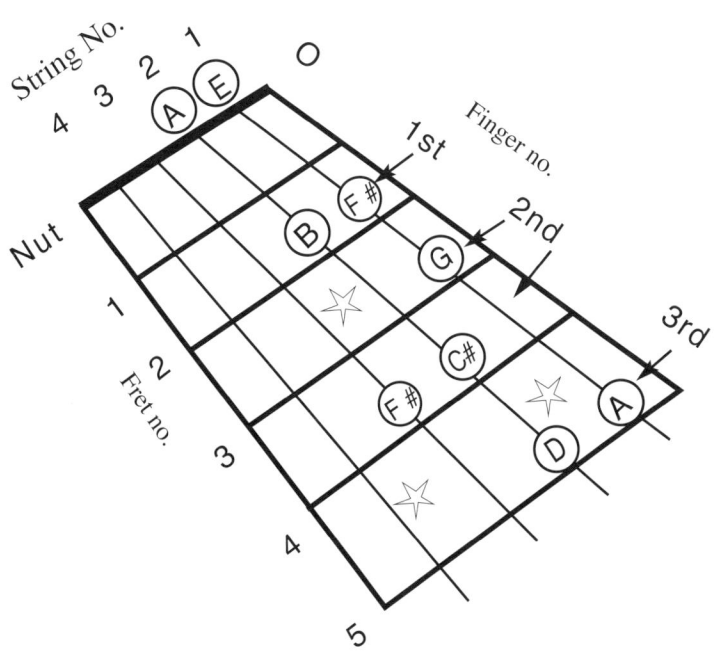

This tune has a different structure of notes which should expand the student's ability, and with a little practice and patience, should be mastered without too much difficulty.

EXERCISE 19
PART 3

Barney Brallaghan. In D Maj. (2 sharps)
3 Part Slip or Hop Jig   Part 3

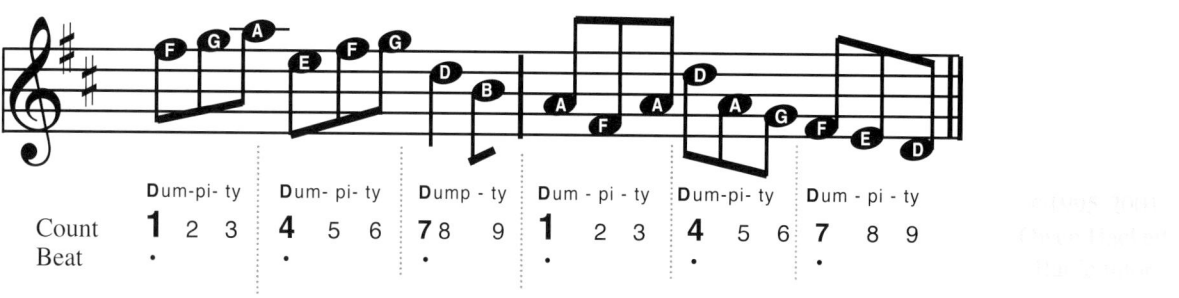

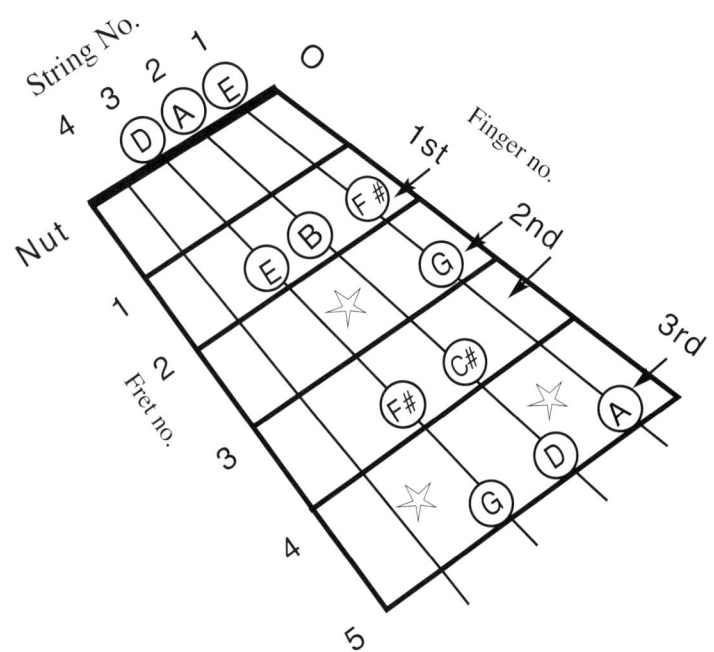

Normally with a dotted crotchet, you could play a triplet and a extra note forming a kind of quadruplet. However, with this type of tune played at a fairly fast speed, you might find it difficult to fit them in. Instead, try holding the note for it's duration (count of 3), or play the note as three quavers. Use both styles.

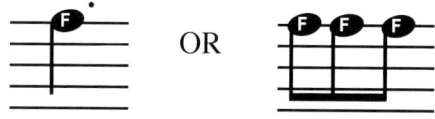

Dotted crotchet can be played like this.

EXERCISE 20
PART 1

49

You have now come the first of the Hornpipes. These tunes have a lovely flowing rhythm, and present the experienced musician with an opportunity to add many varied embellishments.

The Boys Of Bluehill. Hornpipe in D

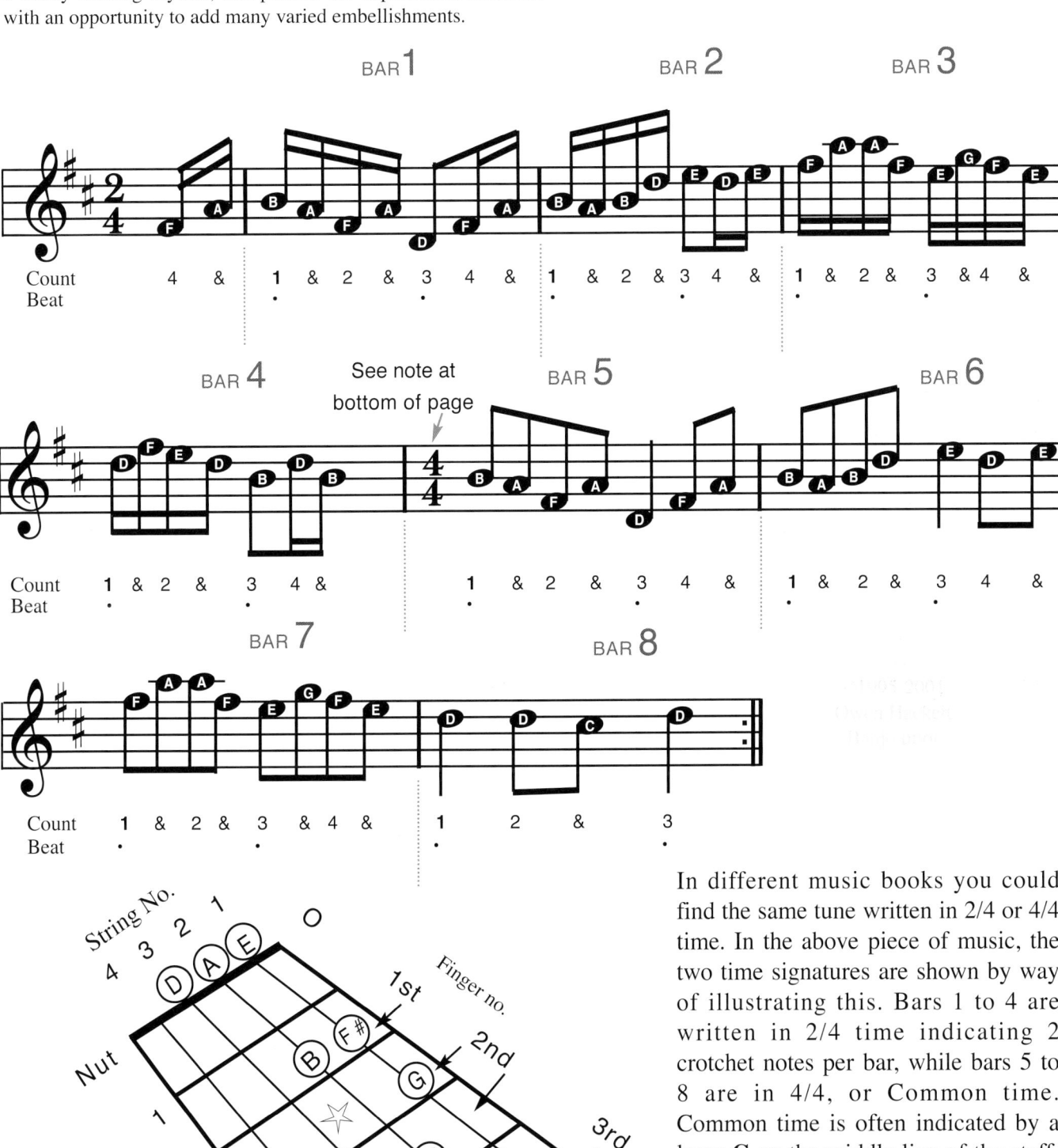

In different music books you could find the same tune written in 2/4 or 4/4 time. In the above piece of music, the two time signatures are shown by way of illustrating this. Bars 1 to 4 are written in 2/4 time indicating 2 crotchet notes per bar, while bars 5 to 8 are in 4/4, or Common time. Common time is often indicated by a large **C** on the middle line of the staff. In 2/4 time each bar totals 8 semiquavers; in 4/4 time each bar totals 8 quavers. Without going into the theory too much, 2/4 time may be a bit more accurate, but both can be used. I find it easier to read and write the 4/4 time.

The tune is continued on the next page.

EXERCISE 20
PART 2

The Boys Of Bluehill. Hornpipe in D. (2nd half.)

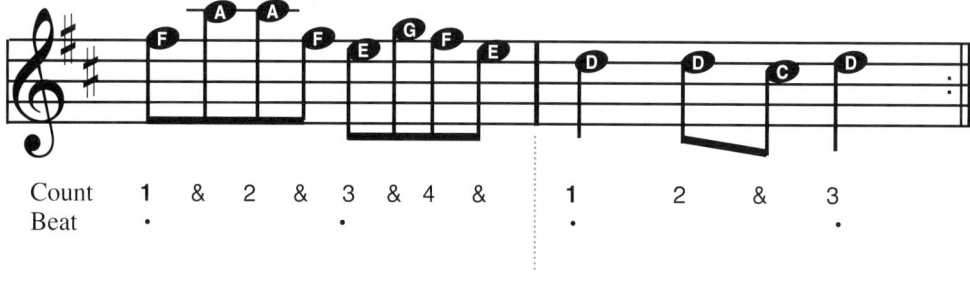

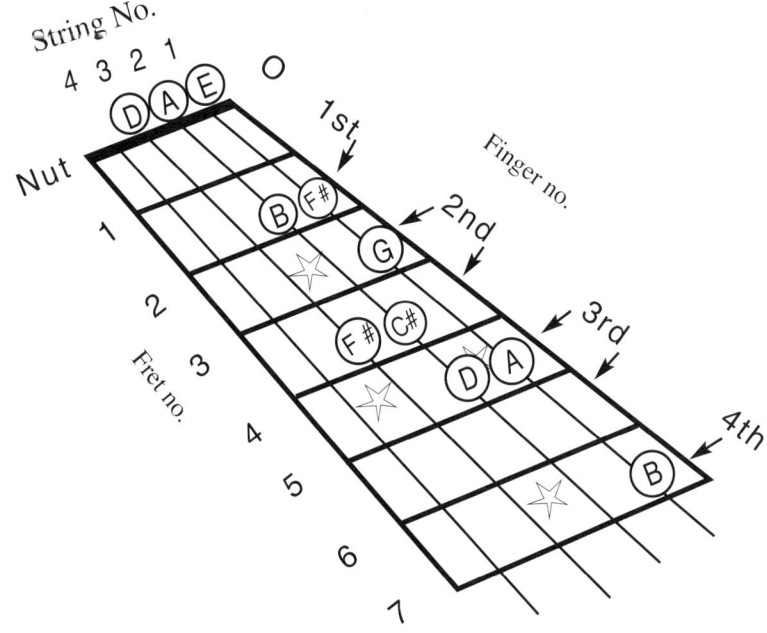

Don't forget to count and tap out the rhythm before playing.

When that's right, substitute the notes for the tapping.

Use the 4th (little finger) as indicated, don't take the lazy way out by using the 3rd finger.

You should try and reach the high B not by moving your whole hand, but by swivelling or pivoting on your thumb at the side of the fingerboard. Always keep fingers pointing back down the fingerboard

EXERCISE 21
PART 1

THE HARVEST HOME. Hornpipe.

This hornpipe will give the student a chance to learn two different types of triplet playing. (Compare triplets in bars 9-10 to those in bar 12 next page). Also if you look closely at the 8 quavers in bar 4 (this page) you see that these notes were turned into triplets in bar 12.

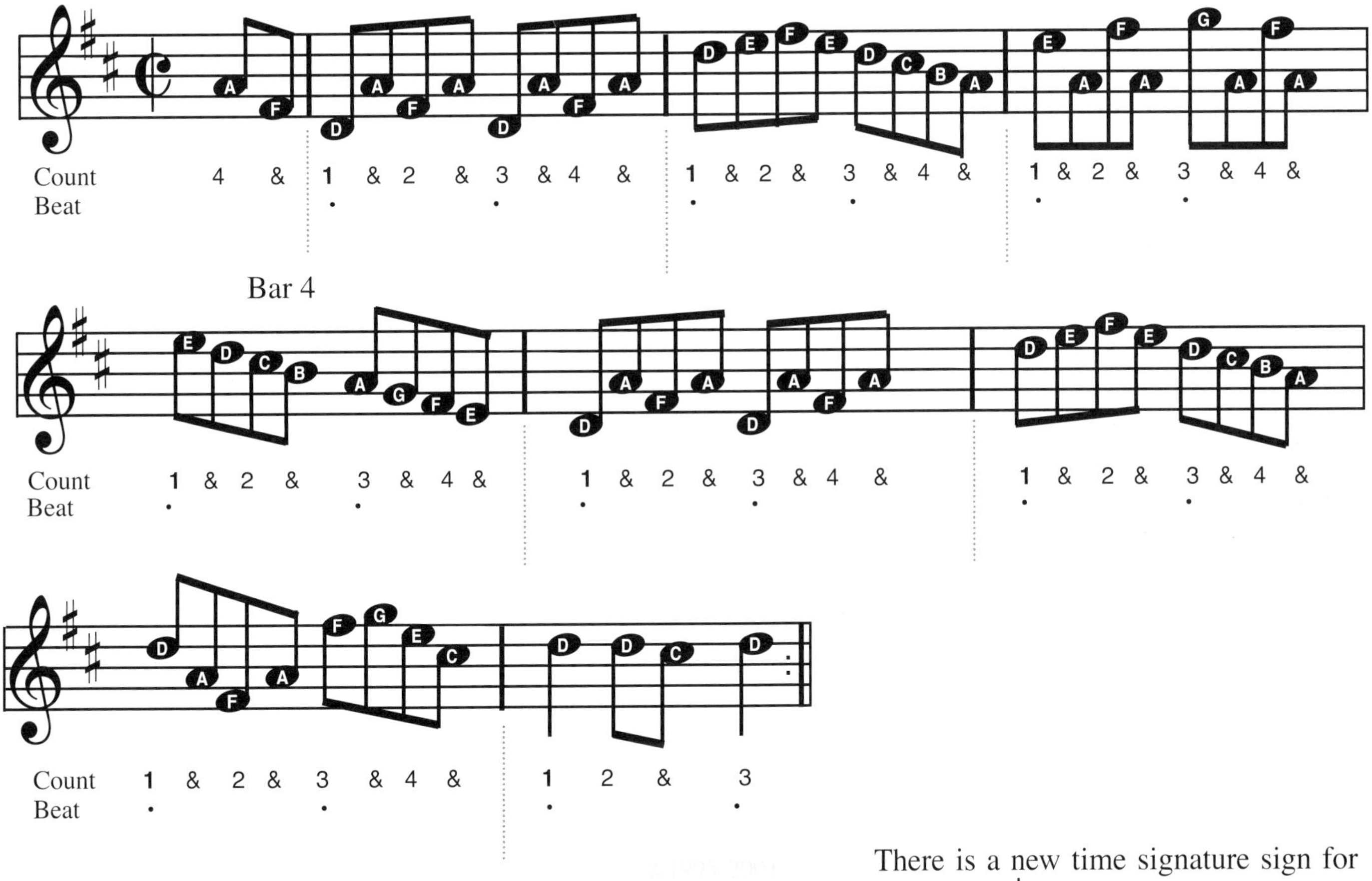

[Musical notation with count beats]

Count: 4 & 1 & 2 & 3 & 4 & 1 & 2 & 3 & 4 & 1 & 2 & 3 & 4 &
Beat

Bar 4

Count: 1 & 2 & 3 & 4 & 1 & 2 & 3 & 4 & 1 & 2 & 3 & 4 &
Beat

Count: 1 & 2 & 3 & 4 & 1 2 & 3
Beat

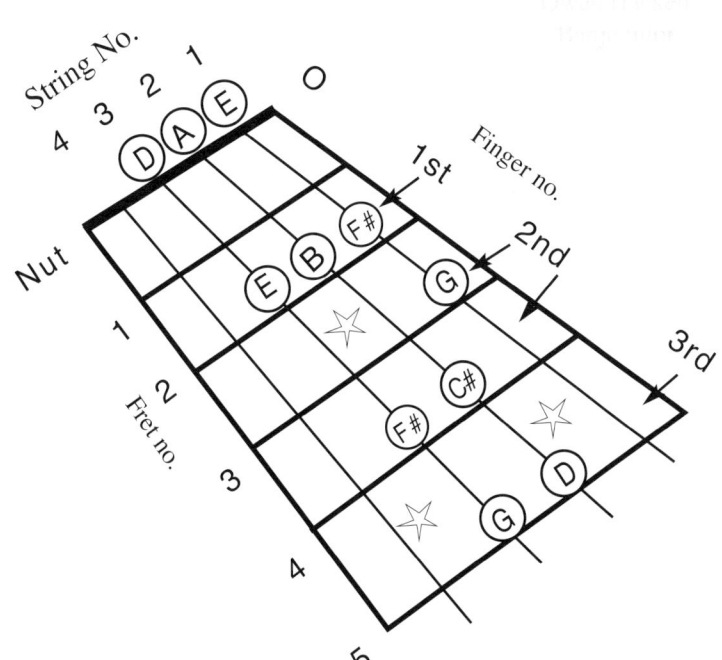

There is a new time signature sign for this tune, ₵. Notice the vertical line going through the large ₵. This means 2/2 time, **not Common time**. It gets 2 minims to each bar, which give a total of 4 crotchets or 8 quavers. It is advisable not to use this sign, as it can lead to confusion. It is only here to explain its meaning, should you come across it in music books.

EXERCISE 21
PART 2

THE HARVEST HOME. Hornpipe.

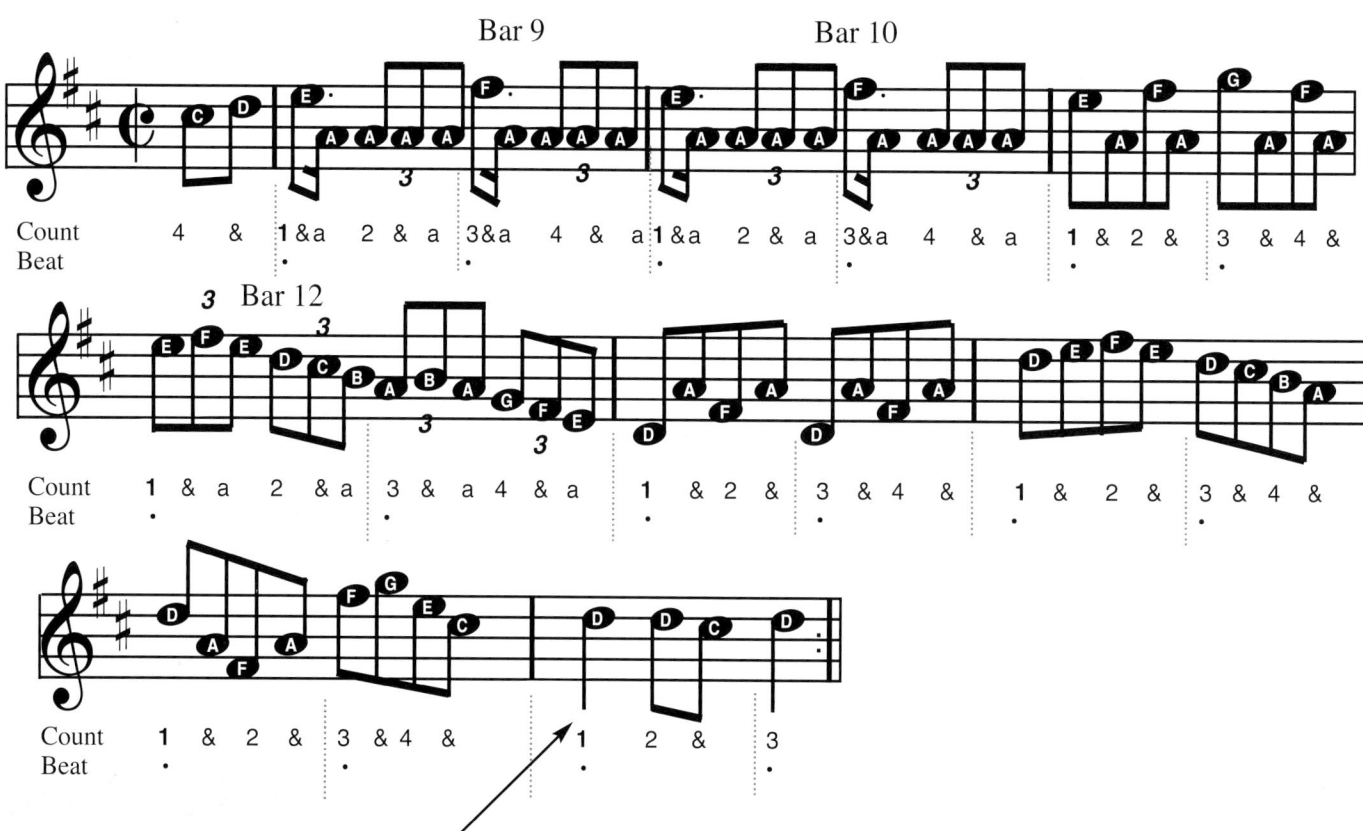

You may treble this D note if you like.

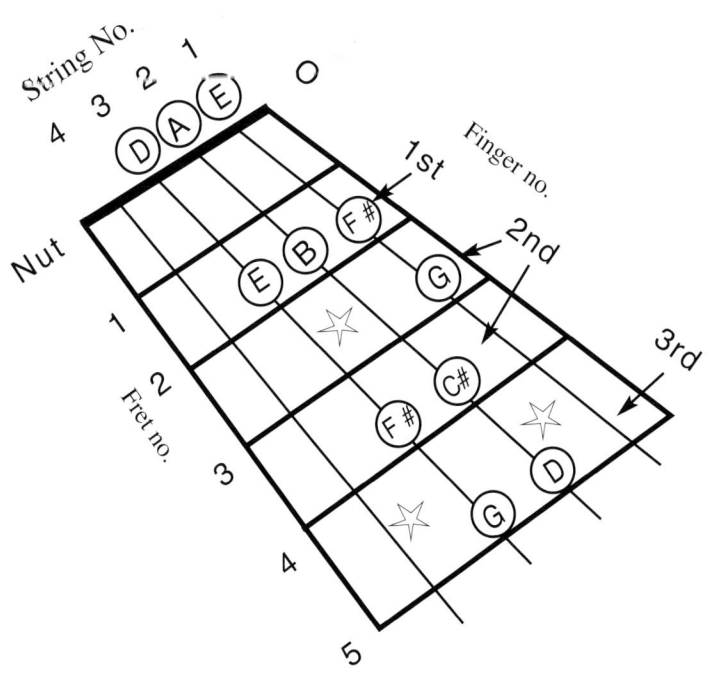

This part of the tune seems at first glance, to have many complicated runs of notes and counting. Start by simply counting out loud **1**,2,**3**,4, tapping your finger at the same time. Do this over and over until you have a steady rhythm going, (not too fast). Then introduce the (&) without breaking the rhythm, **1**&2&**3**&4&. Don't forget to emphasise the **1** and **3**. When you are satisfied with your counting, add the 'a', **1**&a2&a**3**&a4, etc. The '&' and 'a' divides the count, to give you the duration of the corresponding notes.

The little **3** means treble the three notes under or above it. In the early stages of learning, beginners might like to omit one of these three notes and simply play them as standard quavers.

Try and create a smooth, continuous rolling effect with the triplets in bar 12.

EXERCISE 22
PART 1

THE FRIENDLY VISIT. Hornpipe.

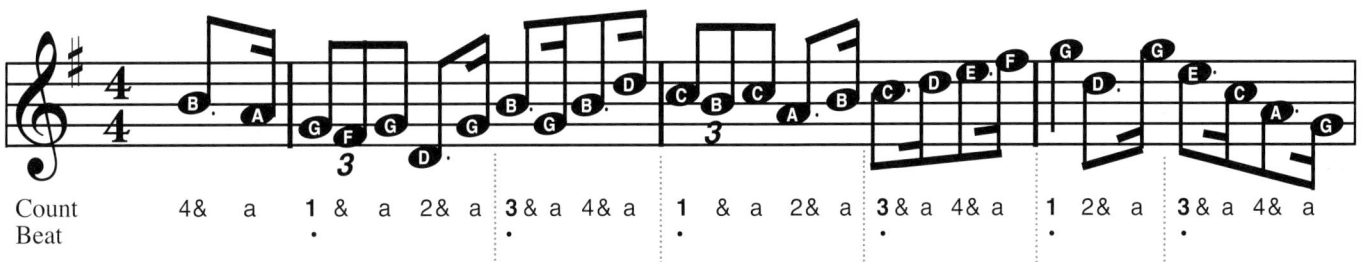

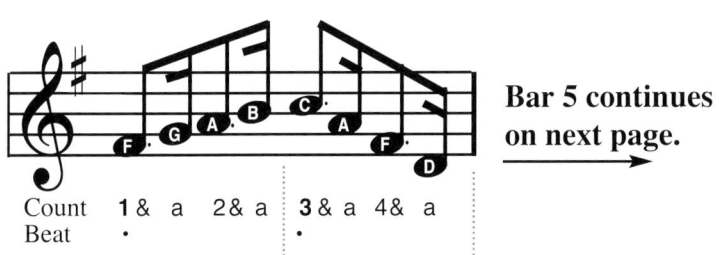

Bar 5 continues on next page.

The dotted Quavers and semiquavers in this popular hornpipe, could at first appear difficult. But we can cheat a little by simply playing them as ordinary quavers for the first few attempts; .
Below is an example of the first 4 bars of the above tune repeated as plain quavers.

Here is an example of the **above four bars repeated** as **Quavers.**

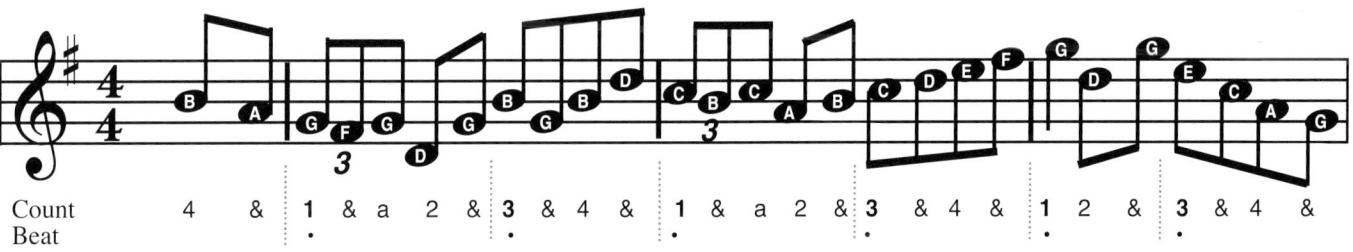

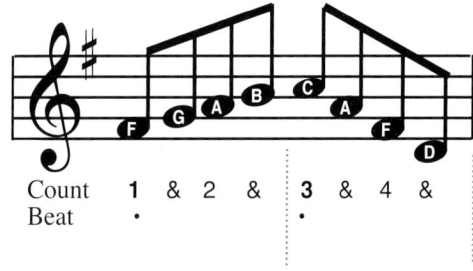

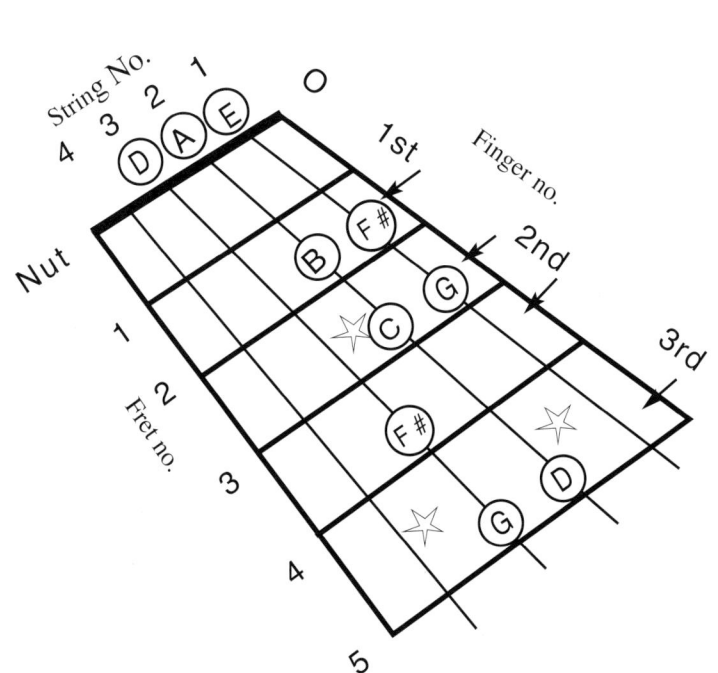

When you emphasise the beat notes they naturally appear to be held for the correct amount of time. Well, almost. The top version gives a more hoppy type of tune, it puts more bounce into it because of the different note values. But most musicians naturally put this into their music even though it may be written as the lower version.

EXERCISE 22
PART 2

THE FRIENDLY VISIT. Hornpipe.

continued from previous page....

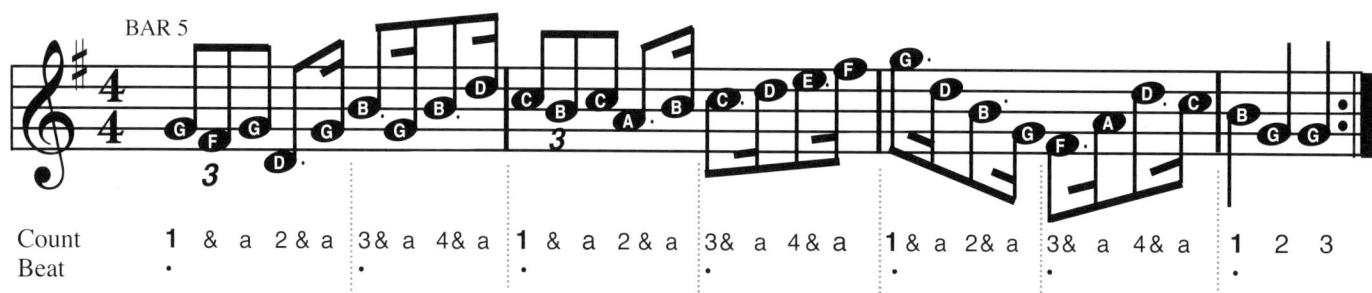

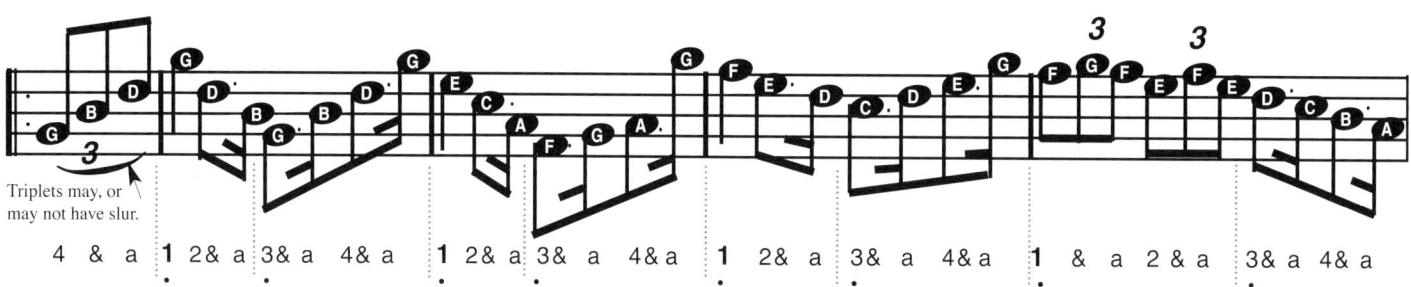

Triplets may, or may not have slur.

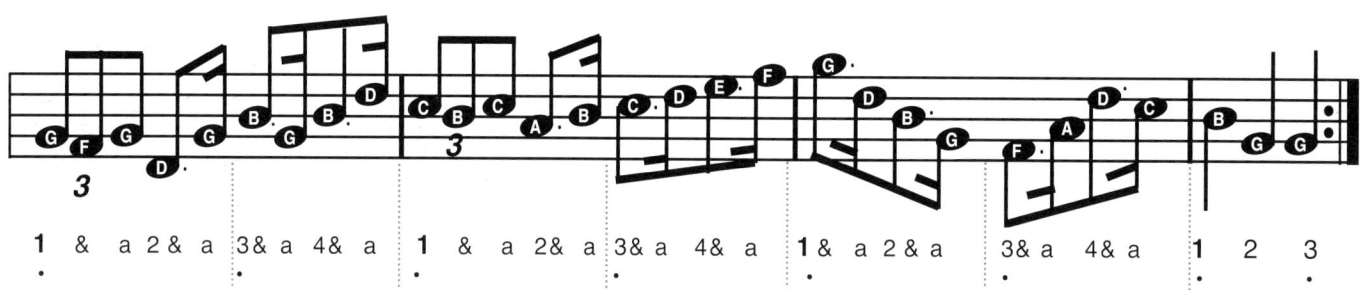

If you look at the middle staff line of music, you'll notice that the first three full bars start with a crotchet. These can be played as triplets as shown below.

For the G; you have three choices

Your choice for E

And F♯

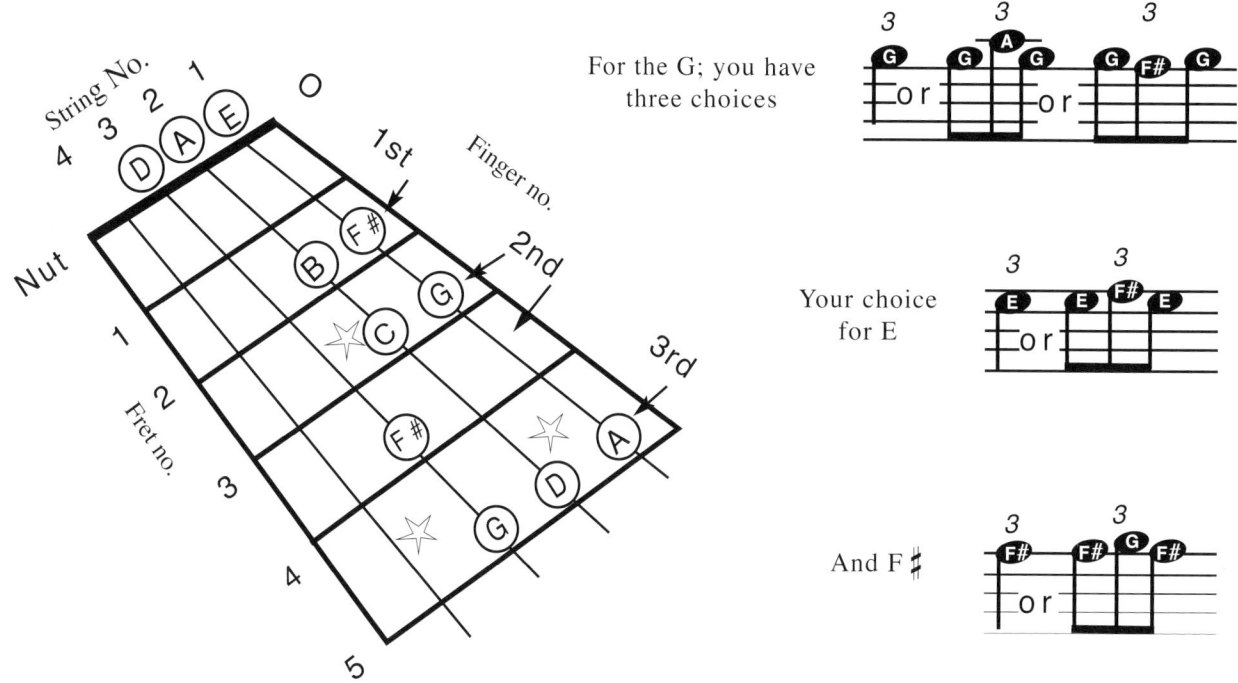

EXERCISE 22
PART 3

THE FRIENDLY VISIT. Hornpipe.

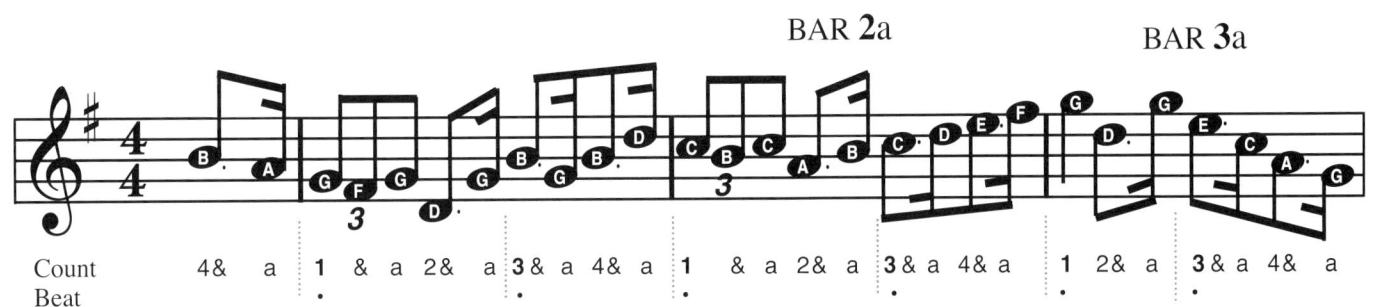

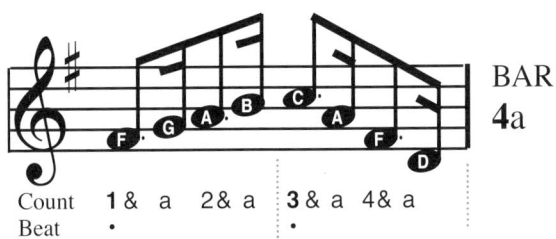

As mentioned earlier, most tunes can be embellished by musicians to their own individual style. As a further example of this, we'll do some work on this hornpipe. If you are only learning the instrument, you would be well advised to leave the embellishing until you have gained some further experience.

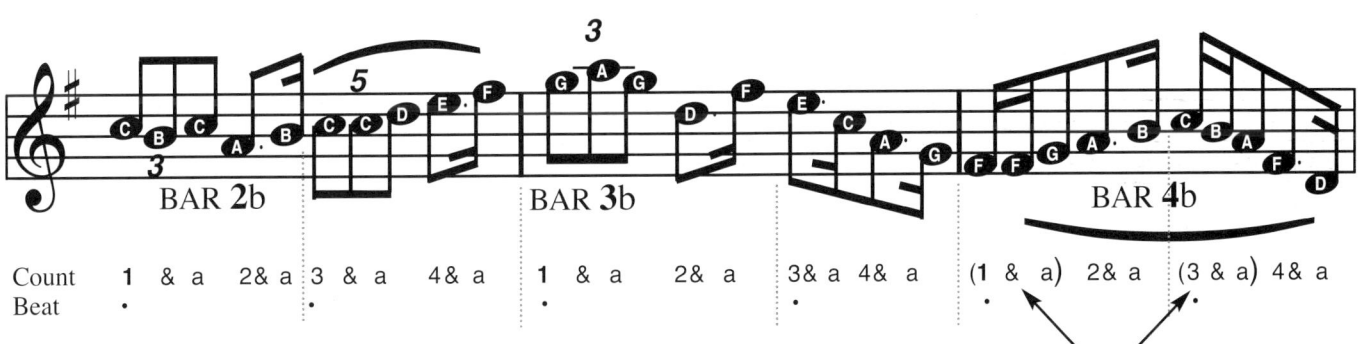

NOTE.. The counting, just here is not strictly accurate, but to avoid complications we'll use it.

Bars 2a and 2b are the same, but the C & D notes in the 2nd half have been changed into a triplet in 2b. The inclusion of the slur, ⌢ in bar 2b means that the whole five notes are played in a smooth continues run.
The G crotchet in bar 3a has changed to a triplet in 3b.
Notes in bar 4a is also changed in bar 4b to illustrate another way you might find notes written. The slur tells you to play the ten notes in one long continues type of roll.

Tip
Don't forget, if you find the dots and extra flags confusing, (A), play them as quavers (B).

At the 1st and 2nd endings of the tune, B, G, G. (previous page), try the following enhancements.

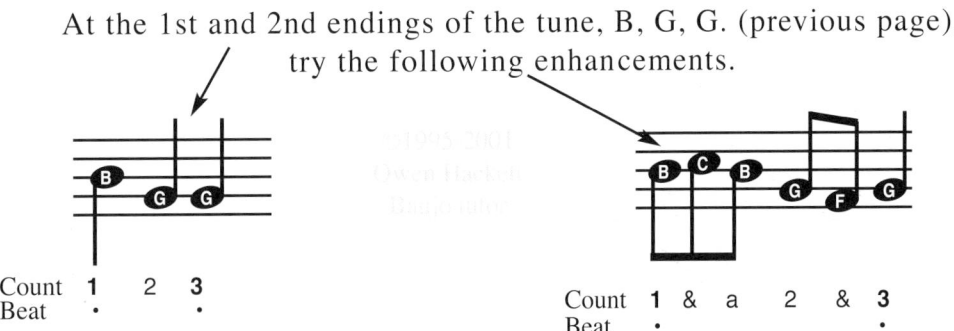

EXERCISE 23
PART 1

THE SWAN. Hornpipe in G.

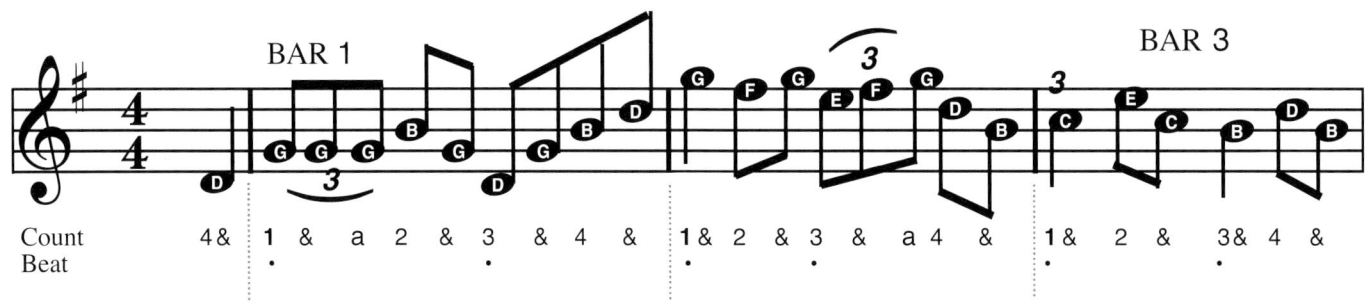

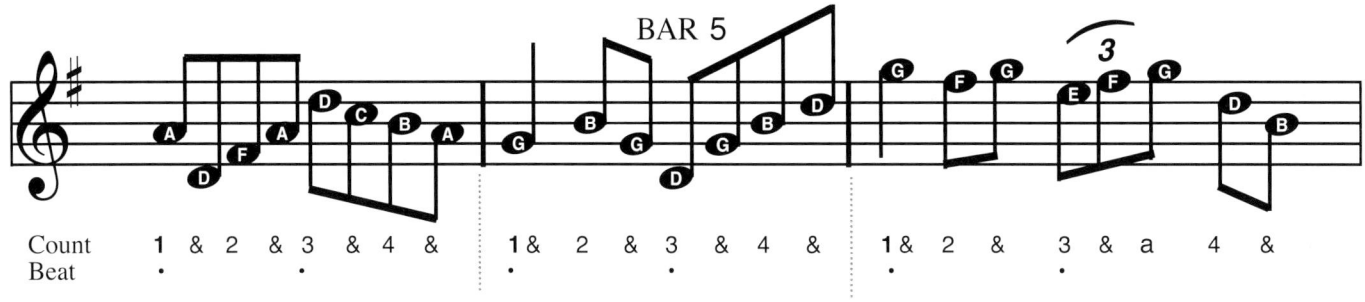

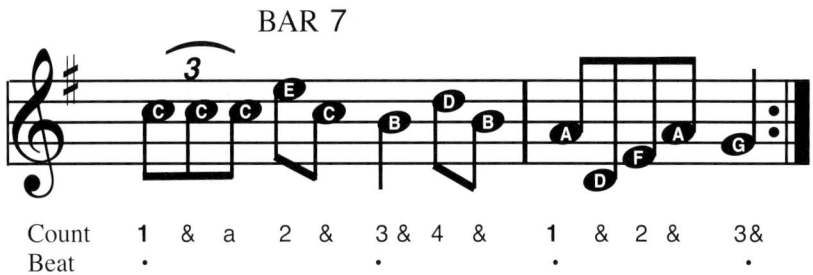

If you look at the counting for the <u>crotchets</u>, you'll see that '&' is added. You don't have to say the '&' here, but if it makes things easier for you, go ahead and try it.

The first four bars are identical to the second four, except for the following:
G crotchet in bar 5 is played as a triplet in bar 1.
C crotchet, in bar 3, and **C** triplet, in bar 7 are played the same, though written different.
What difference can you see between bars 4 and 8?
Where is the missing crotchet from bar 8?
Remember, allow the plectrum to *Glide* gently across strings, especially when trying to get triplets or rolls. If you grip it too tight, this only produces a hard tone.
The very first lead-in note D, can be substituted by a triplet
D, F♯, G.

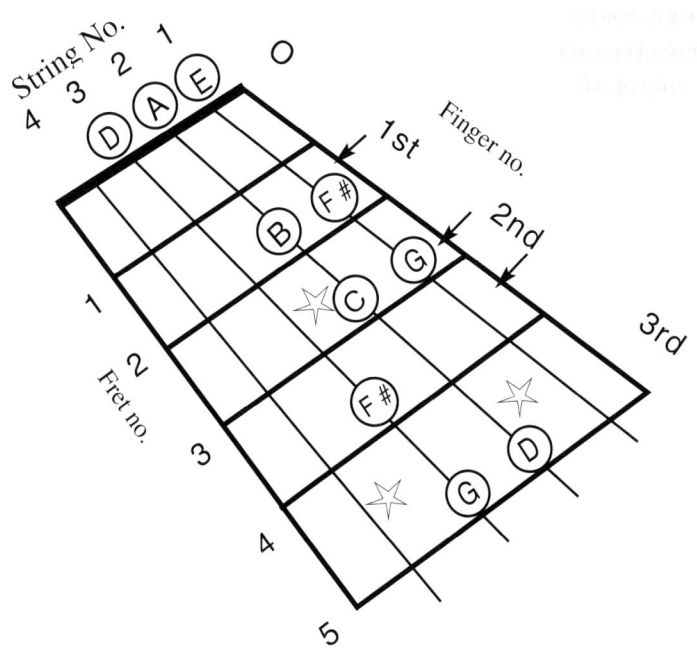

EXERCISE 23
PART 2

THE SWAN. Hornpipe in G.

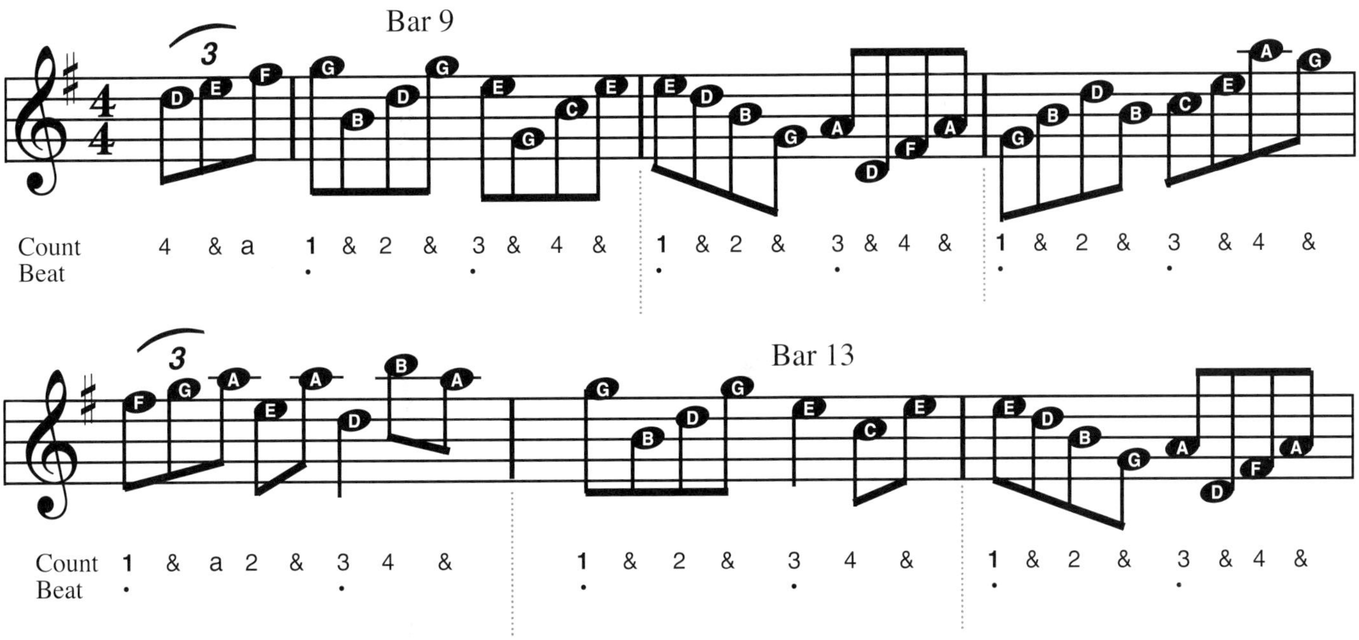

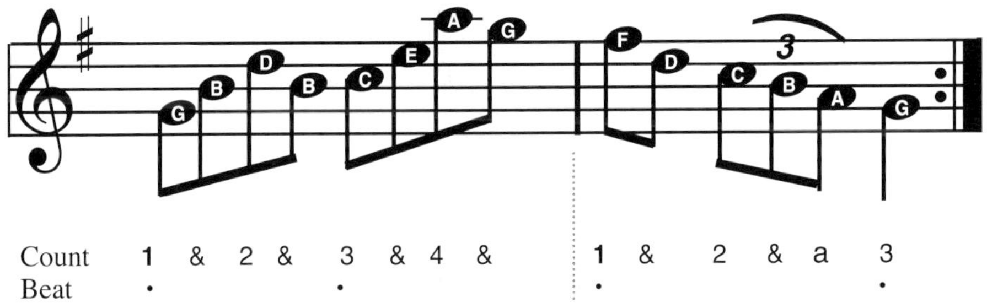

[Musical notation — Bar 9 through end, with count/beat markings below each stave:

Stave 1 (Bar 9): Count: 4 & a | 1 & 2 & 3 & 4 & | 1 & 2 & 3 & 4 & | 1 & 2 & 3 & 4 &

Stave 2 (Bar 13): Count: 1 & a 2 & 3 & 4 & | 1 & 2 & 3 & 4 & | 1 & 2 & 3 & 4 &

Stave 3: Count: 1 & 2 & 3 & 4 & | 1 & 2 & a 3]

Don't get confused with
BAR of music and
BAR to simultaneously
press down two or more
strings on the fingerboard
with the same finger.

(Barring notes) is when two
or more strings are pressed
down with the same finger
at the same time.

Bar 9 and 13 are the same, but in bar 13 an **E** crotchet replaces the **E** and **G** in bar 9. This kind of modification is fine as long as it is done tastefully. Experience helps. In order to reach the high **B** quickly and efficiently, try the following; The note you play before the high **B** is **D,** with your third finger. Allow this finger to rest on the **D** also barring the High **A**; use this **A** as a 'stepping' stone to easily get to the high **B**. When you play the high **B** 'walk' your fingers back along the frets playing the **A** on which your third finger is already resting, and the **G** with 2nd finger etc.

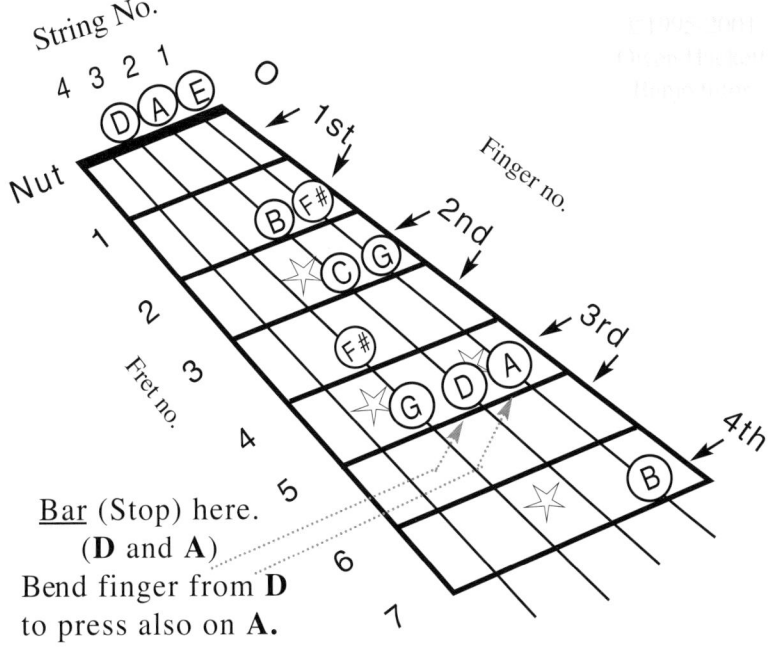

Bar (Stop) here.
   (**D** and **A**)
Bend finger from **D**
to press also on **A**.

EXERCISE 24

KERRY POLKA in D.

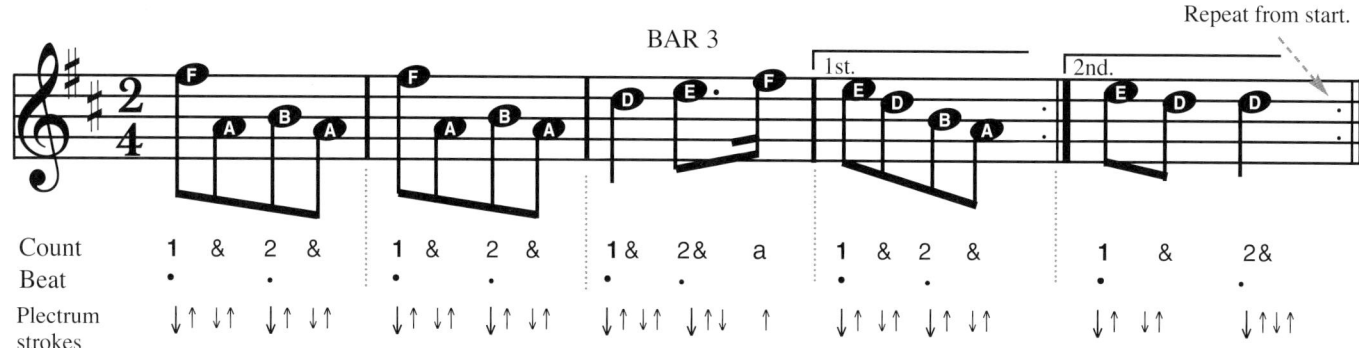

You can see that in this tune the quavers ♪ receive two plectrum strokes. This is not always the case. ie. Jigs / Reels / Hornpipes, all get one stroke per ♪ Polkas too, can be played with one stroke per ♪ but for the moment we'll use these (double) strokes for learning, as they help establish proper timing. A very good example is bar 3 above and 8 below which have a dotted quaver and a semiquaver. These combined have the same value as a crotchet getting four strokes, (see crotchet in the same bar 3, also bars 5-8-10.) Let's look at this in detail.

As a dot increases a note by half again, the quaver, bars 3 & 8 instead of getting 2 strokes, now gets <u>3</u>, and the adjoining semiquaver gets 1 stroke, a total of 4 strokes. As you improve and can play faster, (Polkas are played fast) you might like to omit the 2nd ↑ stroke for some of the notes but NOT at bars 3 & 8, keep to the guides there.

(Continued below)

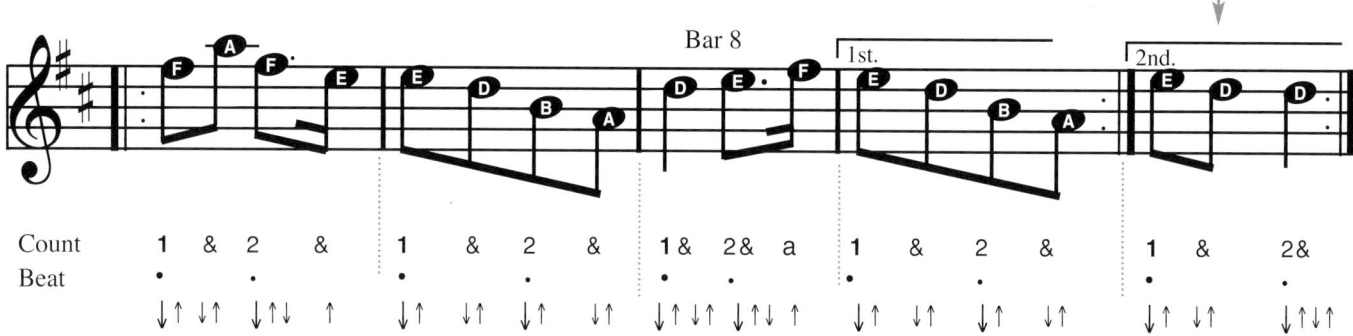

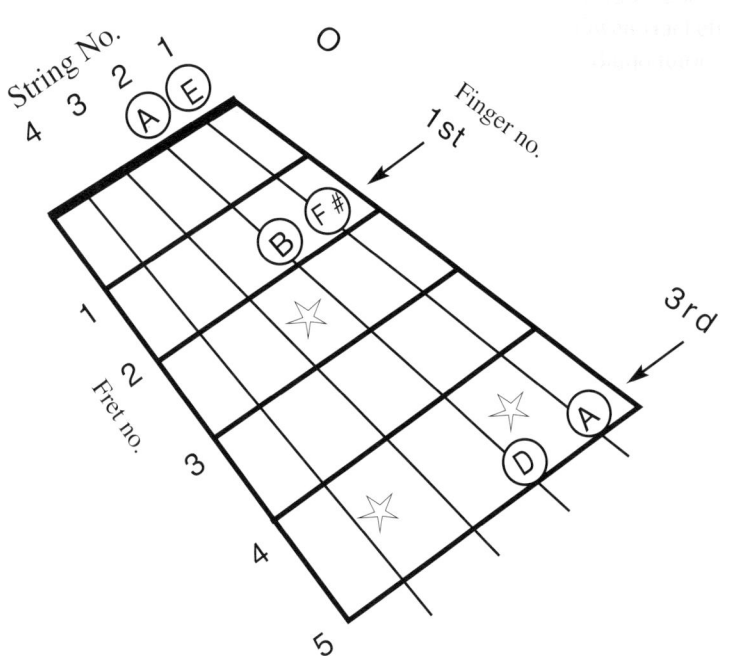

See next tune, Maria's Polka, for more on this. Follow the plectrum guide carefully, developing a steady down and up tempo. Play slowly at first, counting aloud the **1 & 2 &**, as you strike the strings. The heavy arrow ↓ gets the main beat (•). Tap your foot. The second beat comes at the 2, but the emphasis here (•)↓ is not as strong as the first one, but tap your foot here also.

EXERCISE 25
PART 1

Composed by The Author Owen Hackett

MARIA'S POLKA in G.

[Musical notation for Maria's Polka in G, showing two staves with notes labeled. First stave includes bar 2 marker. Second stave shows 1st time and 2nd time endings.]

Count Beat	1 & 2 & a	1 & 2&	1 & a 2 &	1& 2 & a	
Recommended plectrum strokes.	↓ ↓ ↓ ↑ ↓	↓ ↓ ↓↑↓X	↓ ↑ ↓ ↓	↓↑↓↑ ↓ ↓ ↑	
Use these for learning.	↓↑↓↑ ↓ ↑ ↓↑	↓↑ ↓↑ ↓↑↓↑	↓ ↑ ↓↑ ↓↑ ↓↑	↓↑↓↑ ↓↑ ↓ ↑	

Count Beat	1 & 2 & a	1 & 2&	1 & a 2 &	1& 2 & a	1& 2 &
	↓ ↓ ↓ ↑ ↓	↓ ↓ ↓↑↓X	↓ ↑ ↓ ↓ ↓	↓↑↓↑ ↓↓ ↑	↓↑↓↑ ↓ ↓

In the previous polka, we saw how the quavers ♪ are given two plectrum strokes, and crotchets ♩ four strokes. However this is not always desirable. While the note values remain the same, there are many variations of plectrum strokes which can be applied to different tunes. The above polka serves as an example of this. (The semiquavers ♬ still get one stroke for each note)

Above, you will see two sets of plectrum stroke guides.

(Recommended) above the line
(Learning tune) below the line.

Notice there are some up ↑ strokes left out in the upper set; The X also indicates a left-out stroke, (bar 2.) If you were to play the tune fast, as for dancing, you would find the music too cluttered up and lacking rhythm. So when you have learned the tune and mastered the plectrum strokes, revert to the upper line.

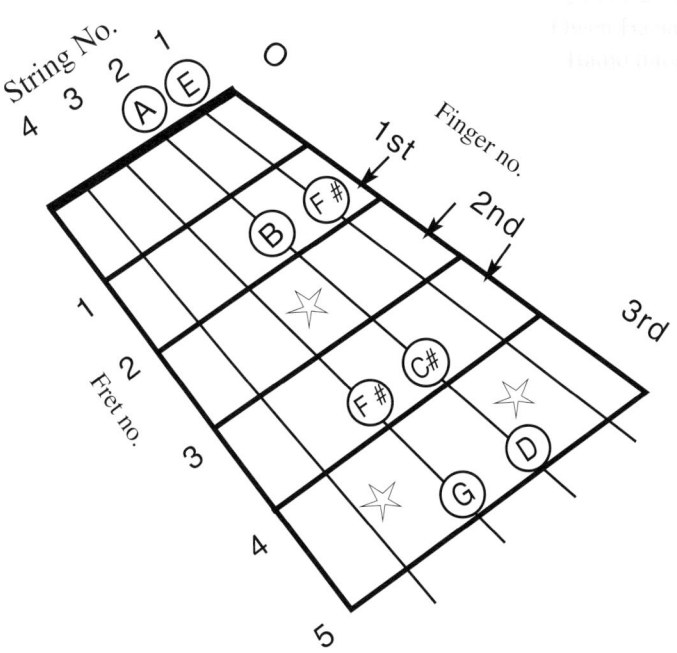

EXERCISE 25
PART 2

Composed by The Author Owen Hackett

MARIA'S POLKA in G.

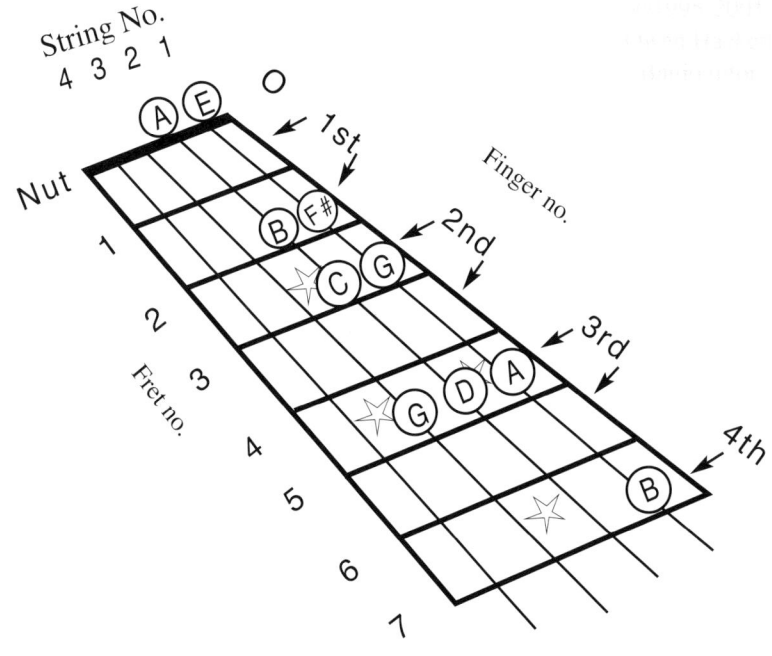

Plectrum guides are given for the top line of music only. The next three lines are similar, but are left for the student to work out.

Most people find it easier to get a stronger beat on the downward ↓ stroke. While this is not recommended in other tunes, as it tends to give a hoppy, boring rhythm rather than fluctuating rhythm, it is fine in 2/4 time polkas.

EXERCISE 26

61

POLKA in A. to get name...

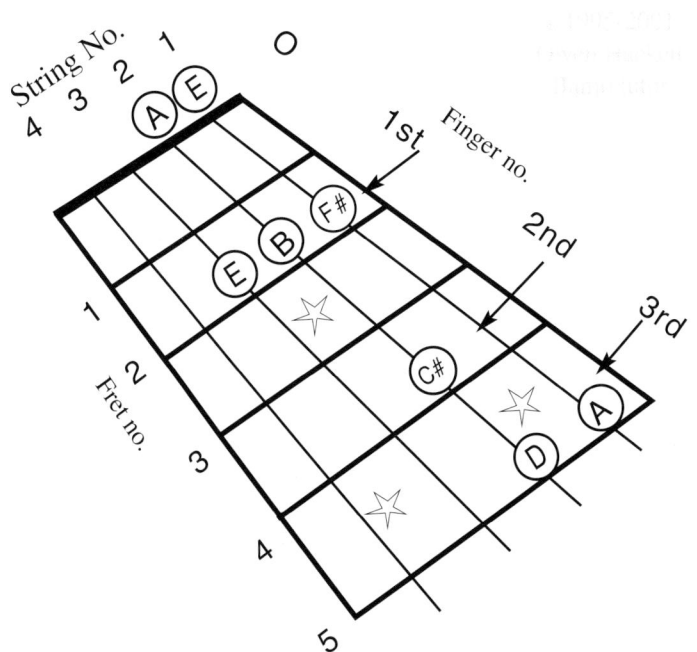

This is a relatively simple polka. However, if you find it difficult getting the timing right, do what was suggested in an earlier polka; play

4 strokes for a crotchet ♩

3 for a dotted quaver ♪.

2 for a quaver ♪

1 for each semiquaver ♫

Play slowly but evenly with a steady tremolo rhythm, only until you have worked out the timing. Then revert to standard picking, keeping to the proper time value for all the notes.

EXERCISE 27
PART 1

CADUM WOODS, Polka.

This polka is chosen for it's difficult note formations which, if the student works diligently, will improve reading and instrument control. Plectrum strokes are given for this page only, the rest are left to you to work out.

In order to get the rhythm right, remember to tap foot at each beat mark (•) fitting the notes into these beats.

You will notice above, that some identical notes receive a different number of strokes. the reason for this becomes apparent when the tune is played at the proper tempo. However, you may wish to experiment with your own plectrum strokes, making whatever changes you find works best for you. If you do, try and maintain a steady rhythm, without any noticeable breaks in the momentum of the tune.

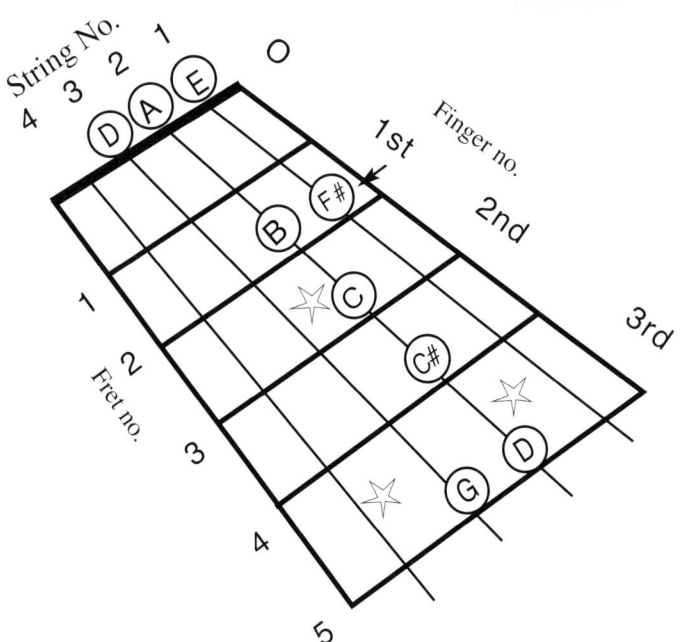

EXERCISE 27
PART 2

63

CADUM WOODS, Polka.

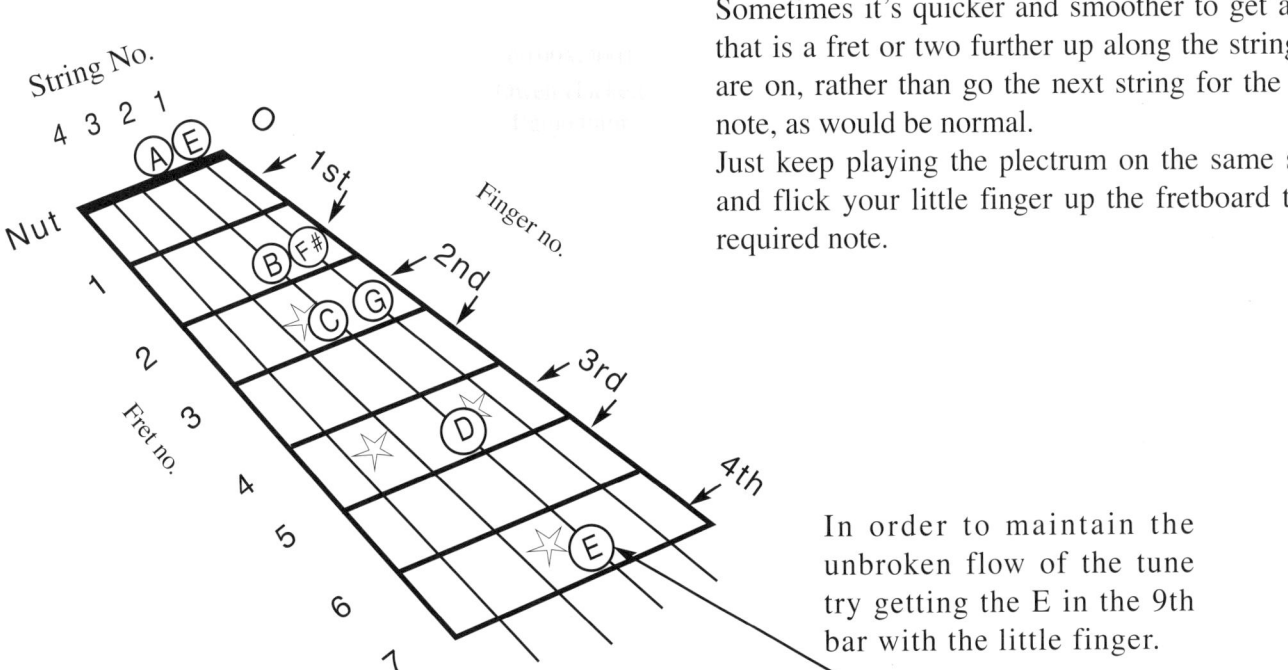

Sometimes it's quicker and smoother to get a note that is a fret or two further up along the string you are on, rather than go the next string for the same note, as would be normal.

Just keep playing the plectrum on the same string and flick your little finger up the fretboard to the required note.

In order to maintain the unbroken flow of the tune try getting the E in the 9th bar with the little finger.

EXERCISE 28

Slide in D.

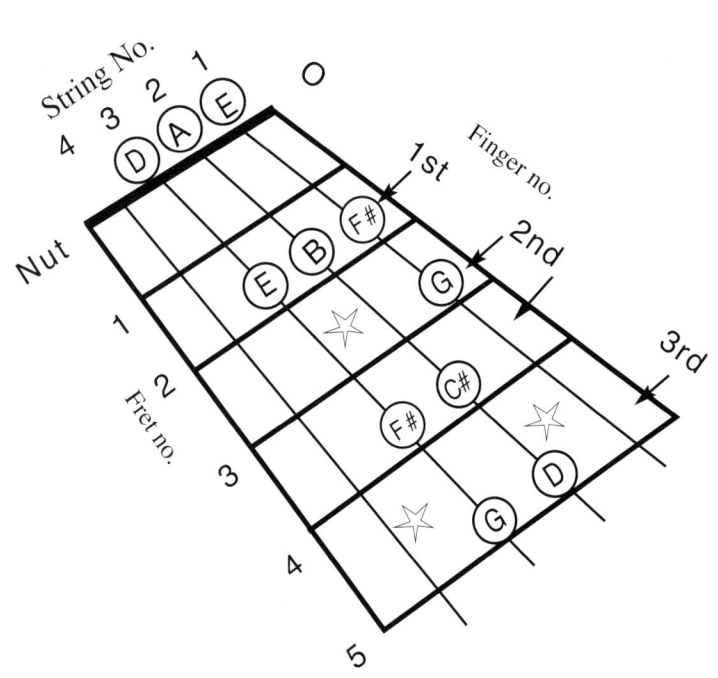

In this lesson we have a slide in 12/8 time. Some slides (like this one) can be played as jigs (6/8 time,. and vice versa. The plectrum is played slightly different than previous tunes in order to be able to get the rhythm right. You will notice that plectrum guides are given for the first line only; if you wish you can use them and apply them to the rest of the tune.

A rolling type effect is needed for slides, and there is very little pause time. That means continuous working the plectrum up and down without a break. While plain and dotted crotchets are shown to have two and three strokes respectively, you may treble these notes. Practice slowly, keeping the rhythm right, carefully fitting the trebles and rolls into the tune without interrupting it's rhythm.

EXERCISE 29

DINGLE REGATTA; SLIDE in G.

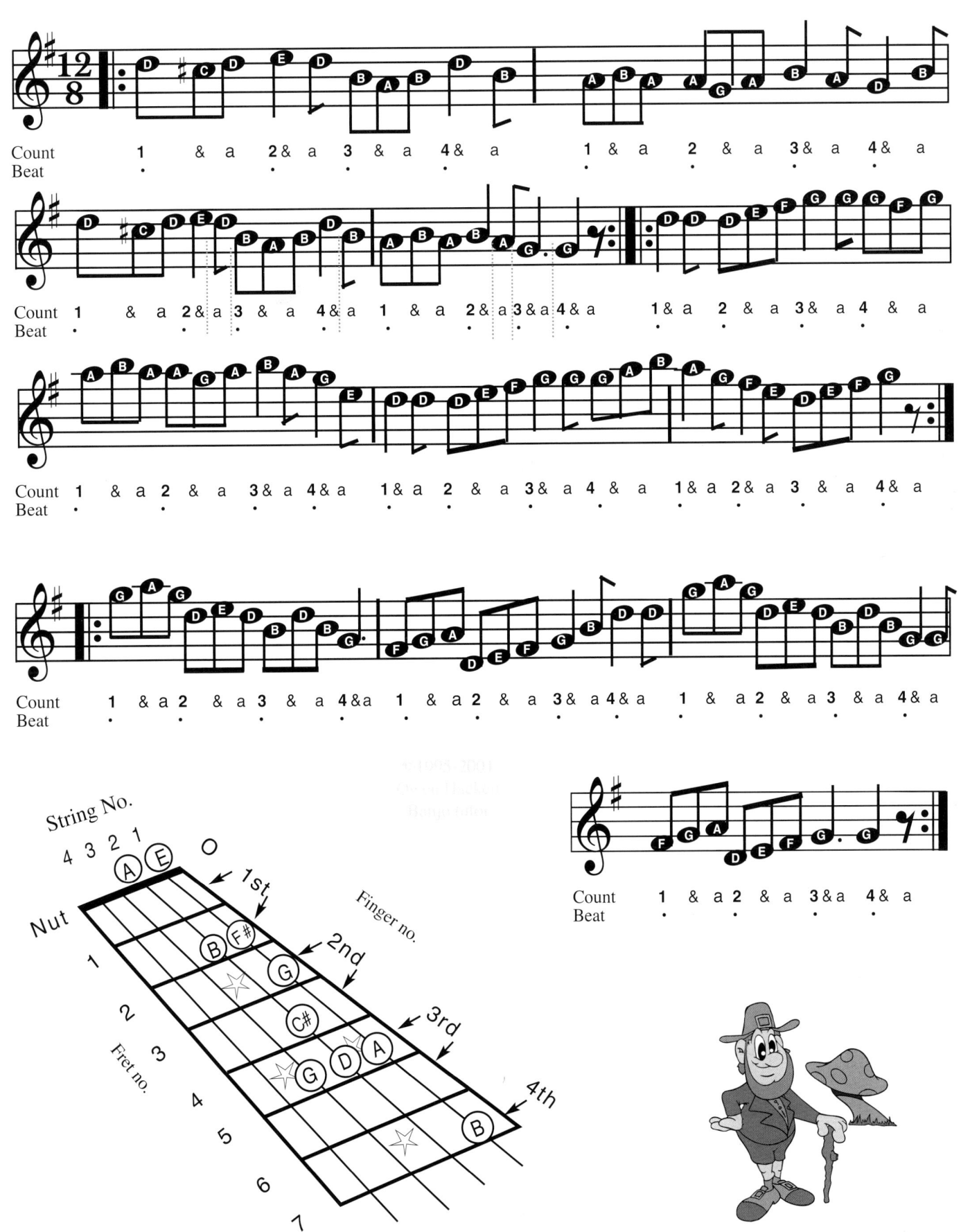

EXERCISE 30

GOING TO THE WELL FOR WATER. SLIDE in D.

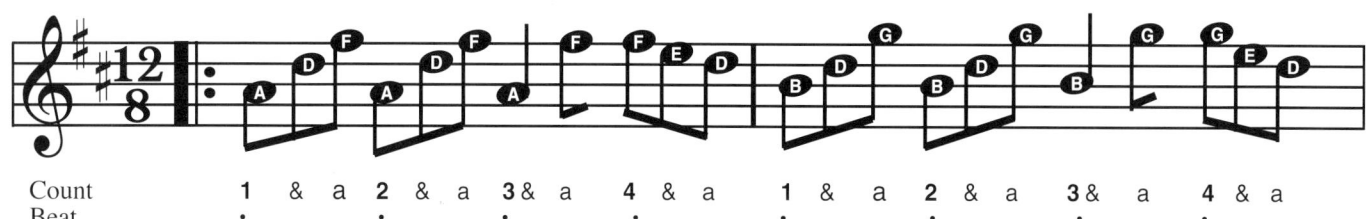

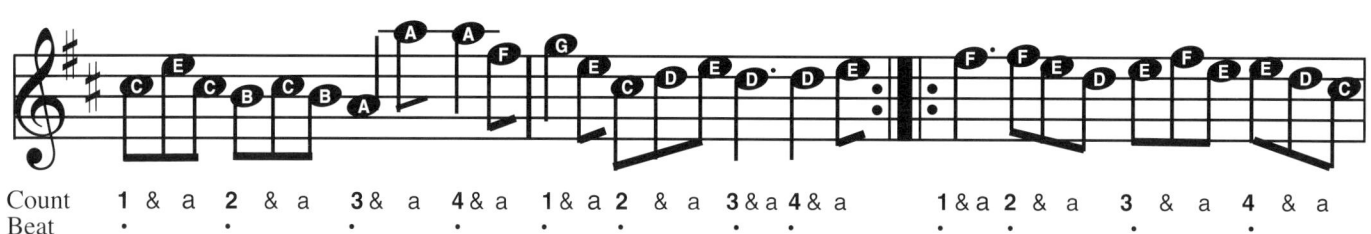

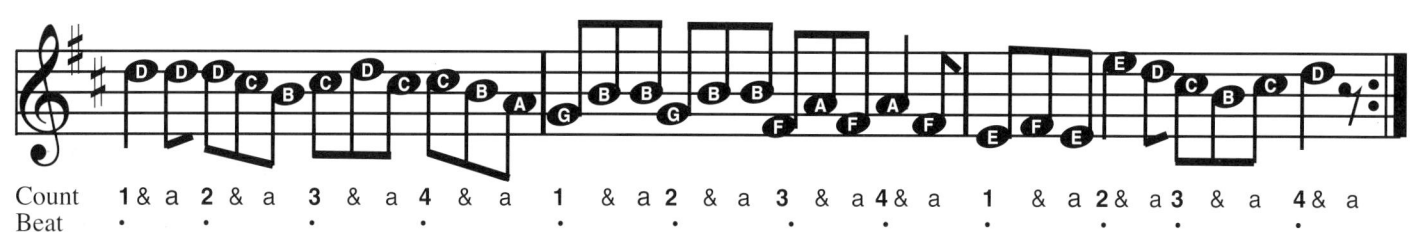

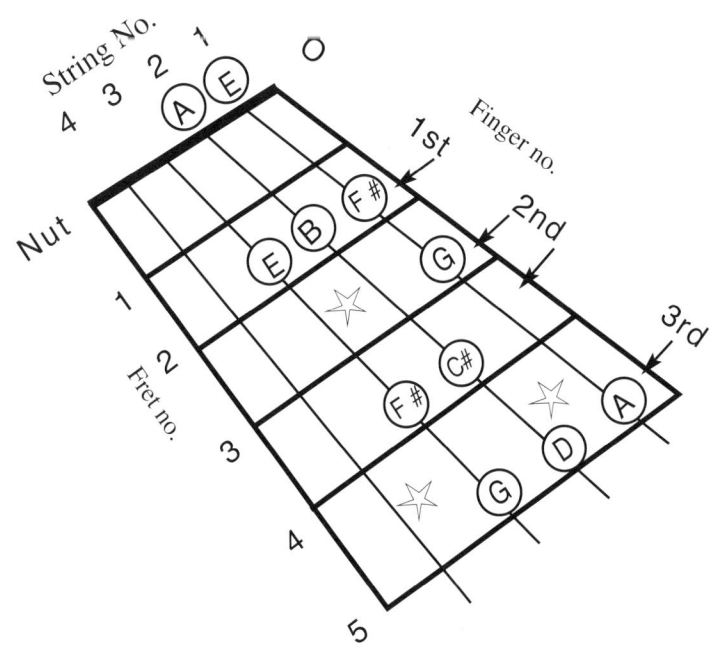

EXERCISE 31
PART 1

TRIP TO DURROW. REEL in D

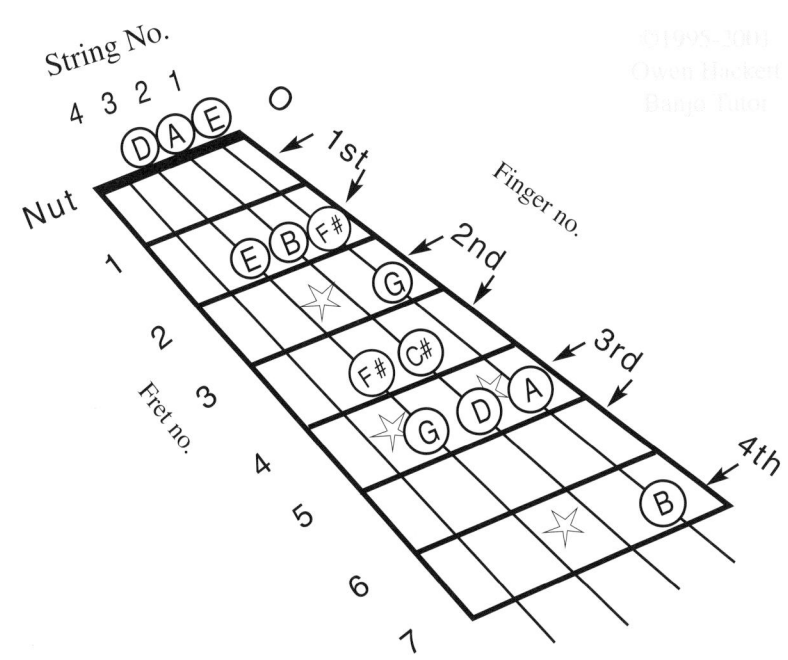

In order to create variety, try playing the crotchets sometimes as triplets.

The third bar is another example of where you could play a triplet by adding an extra note (B) between the second B and the A.
See example.

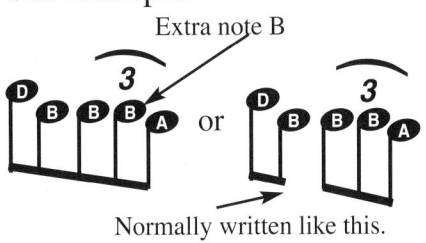

EXERCISE 31
PART 2

TRIP TO DURROW. REEL in D. cont..

In most two part tunes the first part consists of eight bars doubled, or sixteen bars *not* doubled. The same applies for the second part of the tune. This is not always the case, but is the most usual setting of Irish dance tunes.

This tune however is commonly played with the second part, already sixteen bars, being repeated, thus giving thirty two bars for the second part.

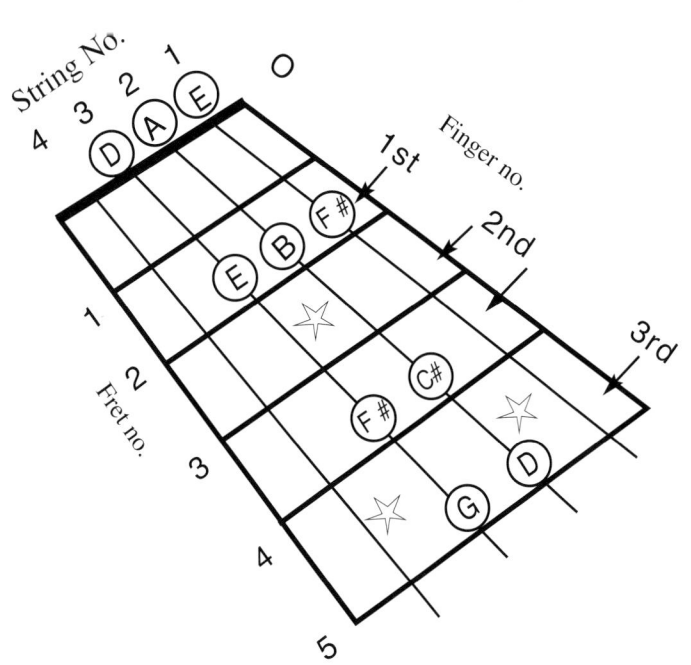

EXERCISE 32
PART 1

69

BUNCH OF KEYS Reel in G.

[Musical notation with count/beat markings throughout]

Accidentals only affect notes in current bar.

In 4th bar of music, (and similar), <u>BAR</u> these notes F natural and C natural, (2nd finger) keeping them <u>BARRED</u> while playing them and D (preferably with 3rd finger.)

In 2nd bar of music, and similar, <u>BAR</u> these notes G & D, (3rd finger) keeping them <u>BARRED</u> while playing them and the high B.

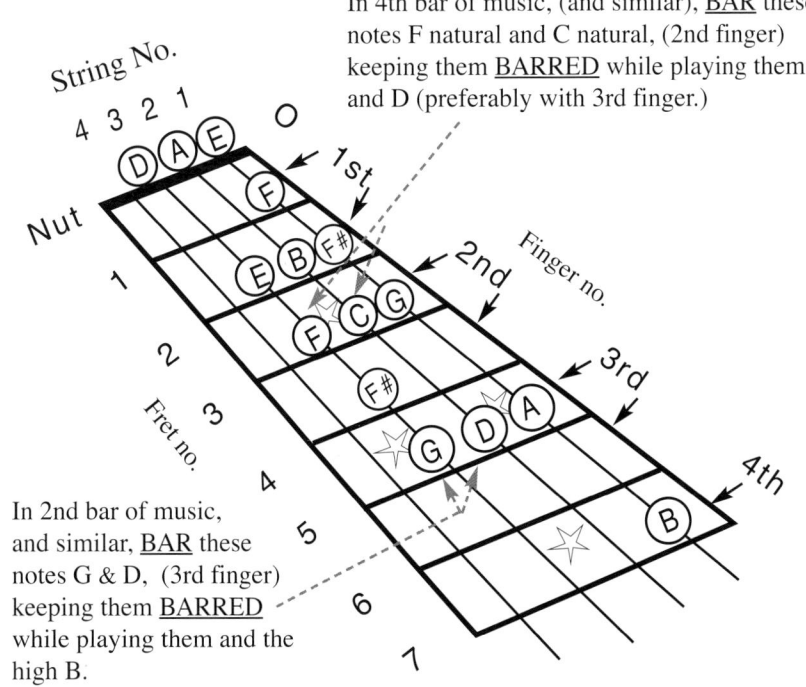

In this tune, we introduce some new notes. ie, F natural, F sharp, C natural, C sharp. For the beginner, this can lead to confusion, so take your time, and find where the notes are on your instrument BEFORE attempting the tune. Remember to use the proper fingering especially on the high notes. The crotchets may be trebled or simply held for duration as you prefer.

LESSON 32
PART 2

BUNCH OF KEYS Reel in G. cont..

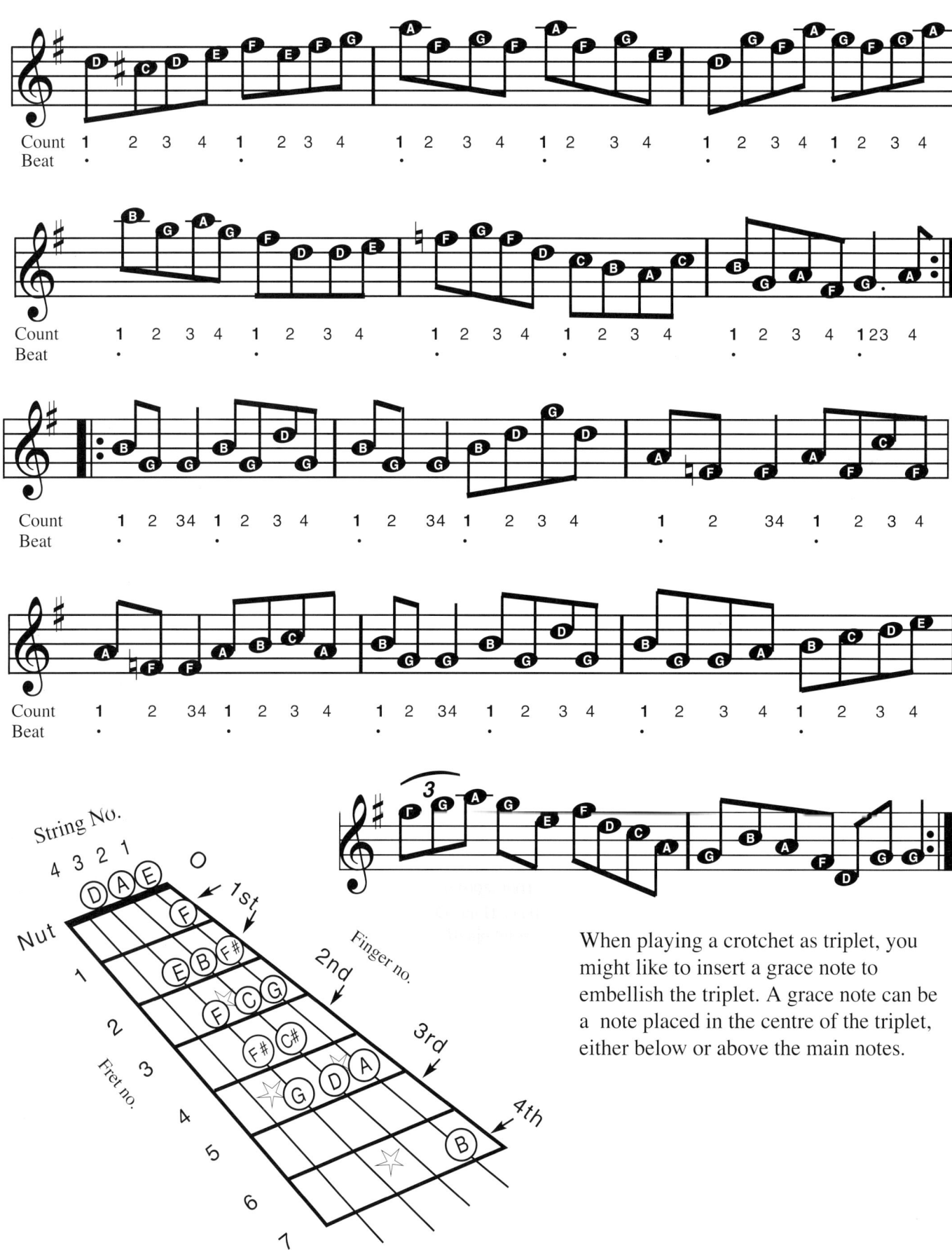

When playing a crotchet as triplet, you might like to insert a grace note to embellish the triplet. A grace note can be a note placed in the centre of the triplet, either below or above the main notes.

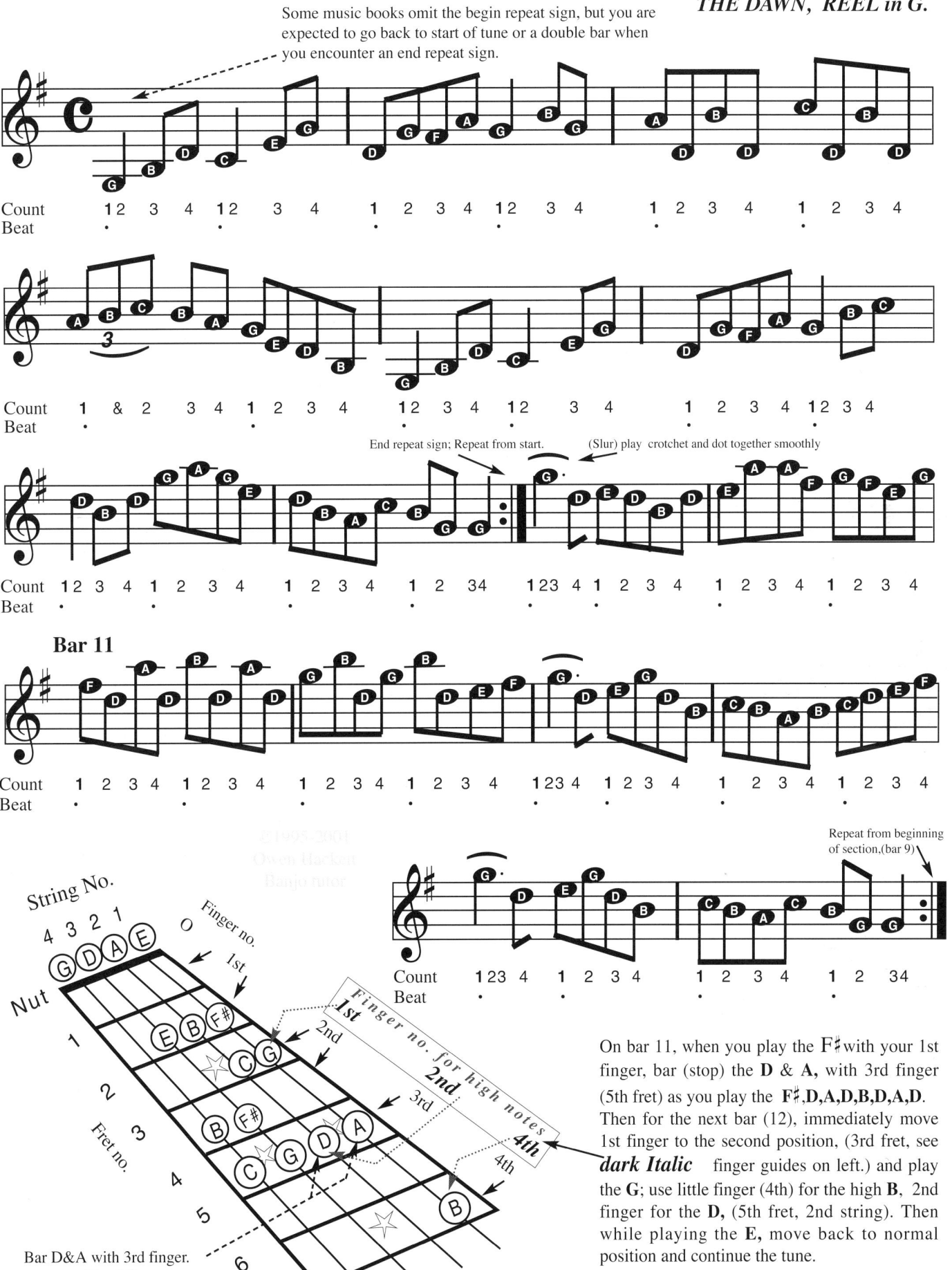

EXERCISE 34

COME WEST ALONG THE ROAD REEL, in G.

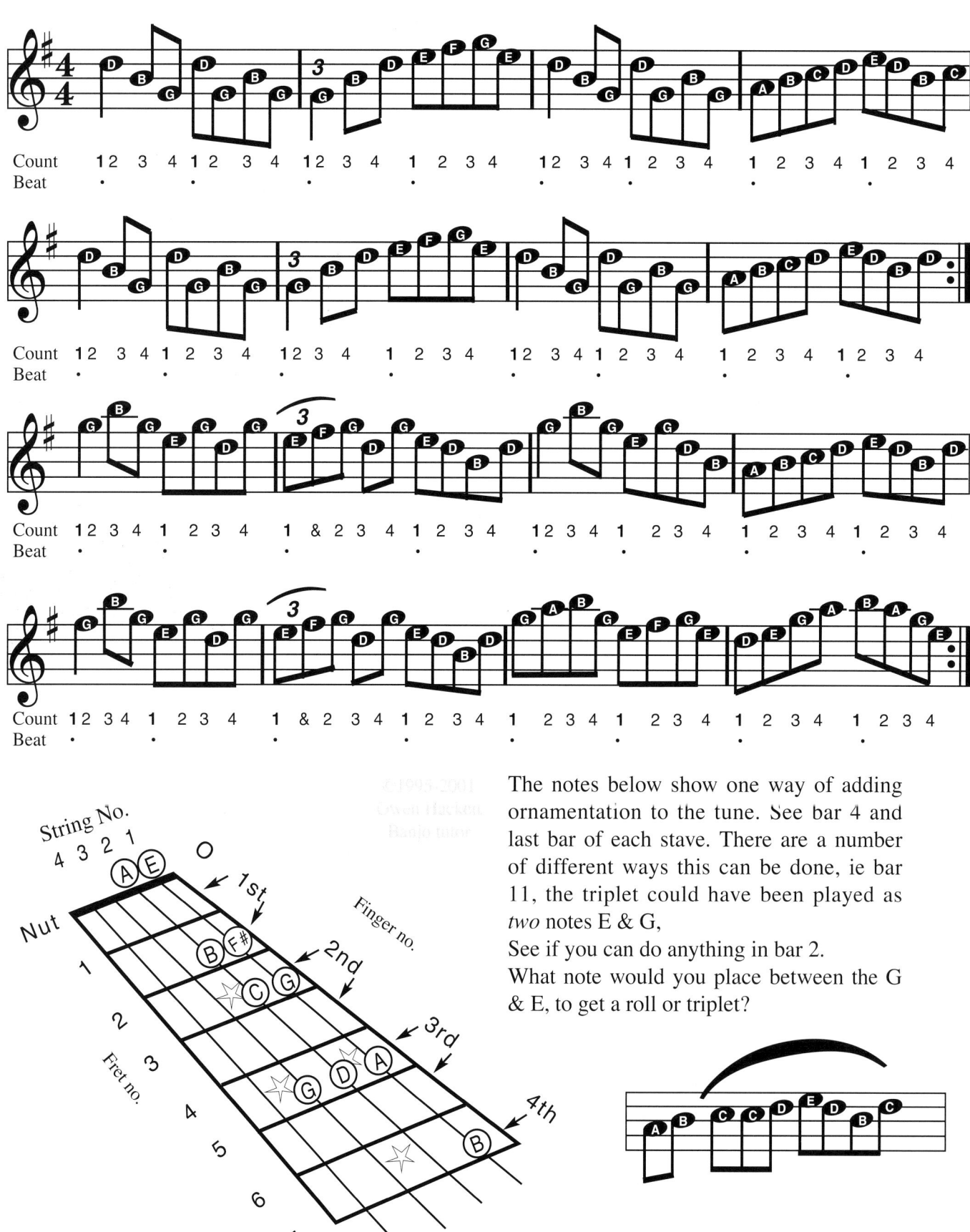

EXERCISE 35

TERESA'S SMILE reel in G.   Composed by author Owen Hackett

Bar 4; (See notes below).

[Sheet music staves with note names labeled on each notehead; count/beat numbers below each staff]

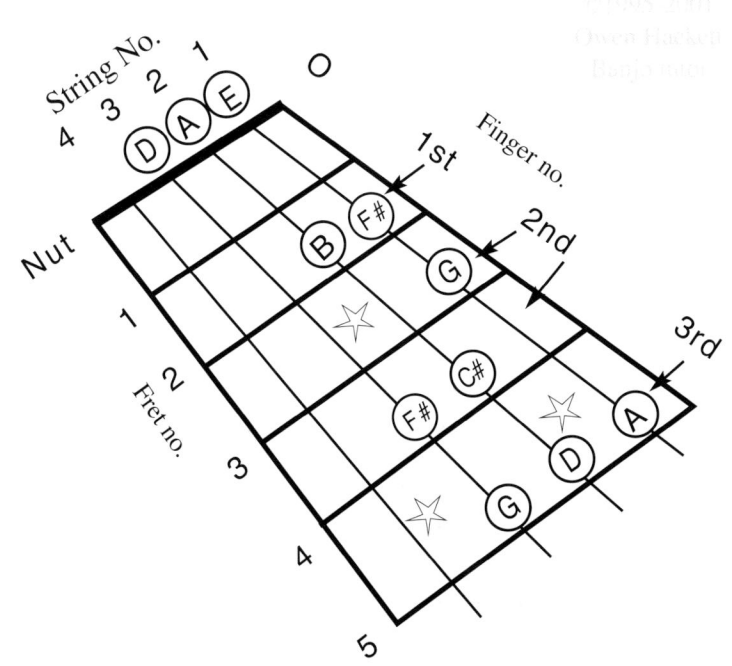

Notice that the Treble sign, plus Key and Time signatures are now only displayed on the first staff. This is usual in many music books.

Can you remember the function of the tie at the last two G's above? See Spancill Hill page 29.

At bar 4 above, you could insert a B between the C & A, to make a triplet. For details refer to Come West Along the Road. (Previous Page).

Don't forget you can treble the crotchets, but in bars 1 & 5 <u>don't</u> treble the first high G.

EXERCISE 36

THE INNOCENT CHILD. REEL in C. Composed by the author, Owen Hackett

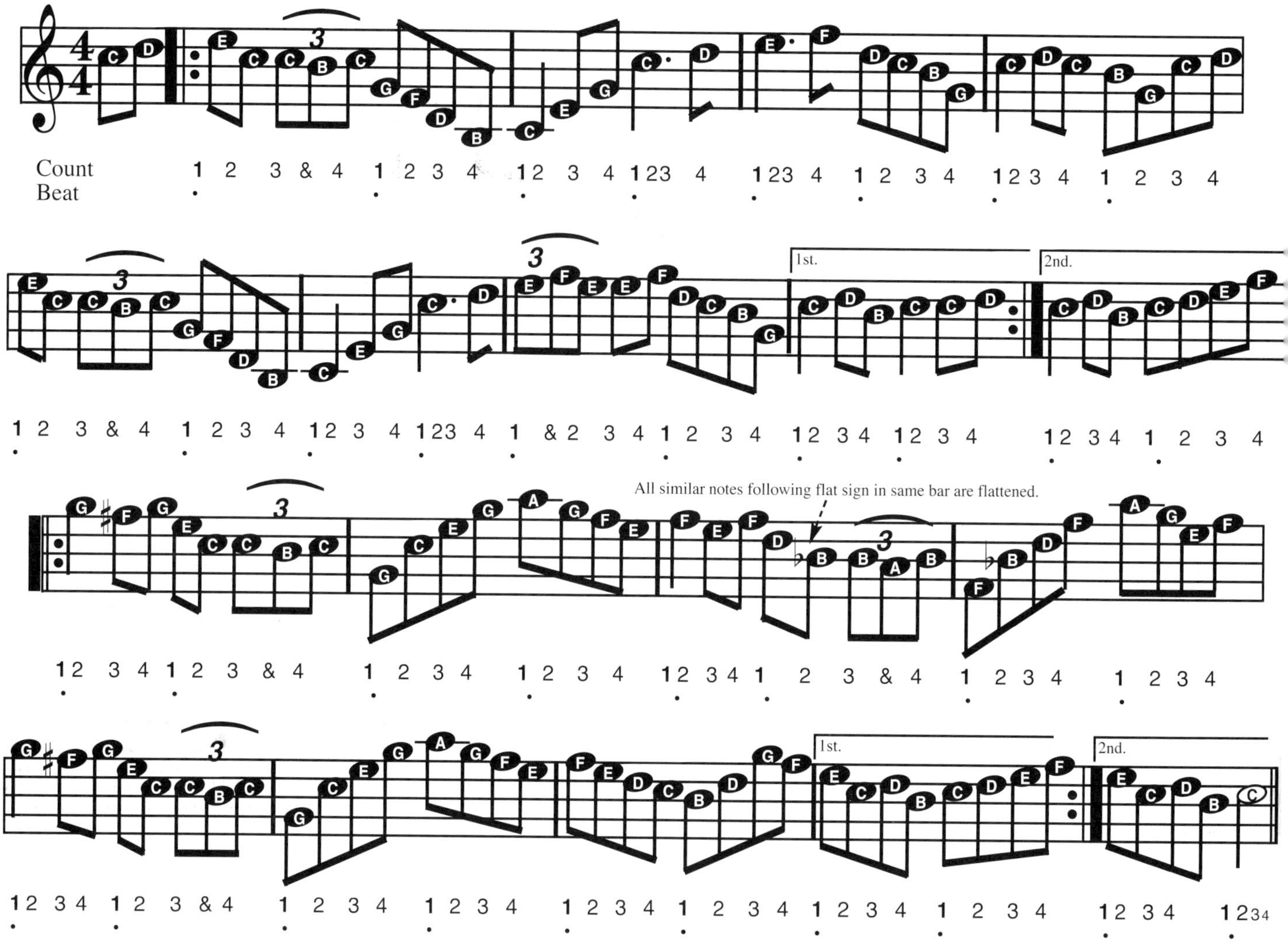

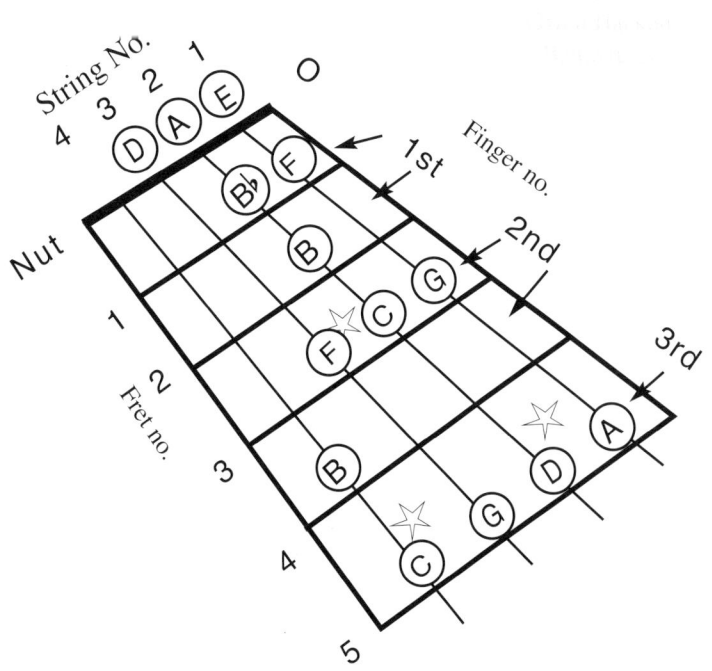

Notes that are sharpened or flattened in a tune OTHER than those in the key signature, are called accidentals. An accidental sign (♯, ♭, ♮) before a note affects all similar notes in the same bar, ie. each F, B, etc. UNLESS it is cancelled by another sign in the same bar.

I wrote this tune in C, which I think sounds nice. But I find it easier to play in D, because of the long neck on my banjo. If you find it hard to manage in C, simply transpose it up one note to key D. Some players can do this mentally as they look at the music, others might transpose it on to a sheet of music paper.
See 'HOW TO TRANSPOSE' in the index.

EXERCISE 37

75

Composed by the author

The Retreat Reel in D min.

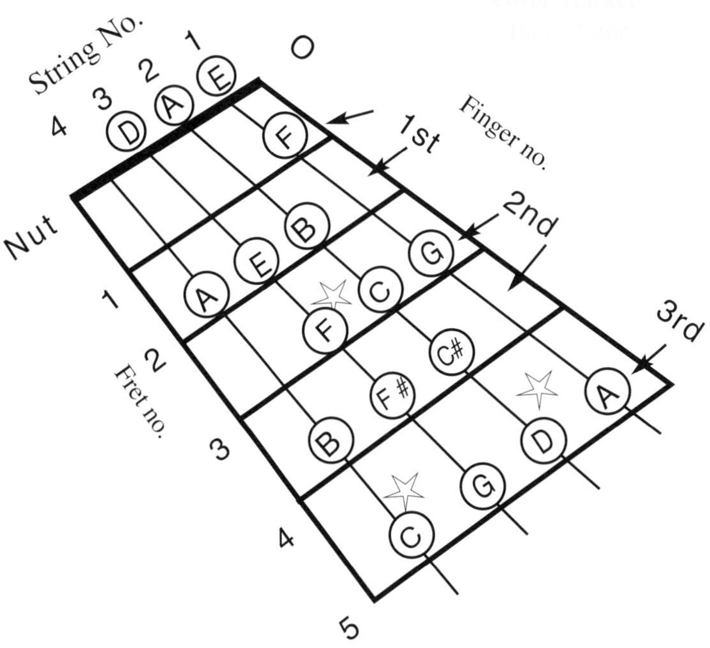

If you find it difficult to get the triplets as written, play each as a D, triplet until you get the tune off. That way, you will be staying on the same string.

When you are going to the high 'A' from the D, (1st bar last two lines), try leaving your 3rd finger on the D, and roll it over onto the A.

For variety, you might like to play a C♯, instead of the last A, in 2nd bar, 3rd line.

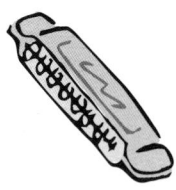

EXERCISE 38
PART 1

John Brady's March, in G.

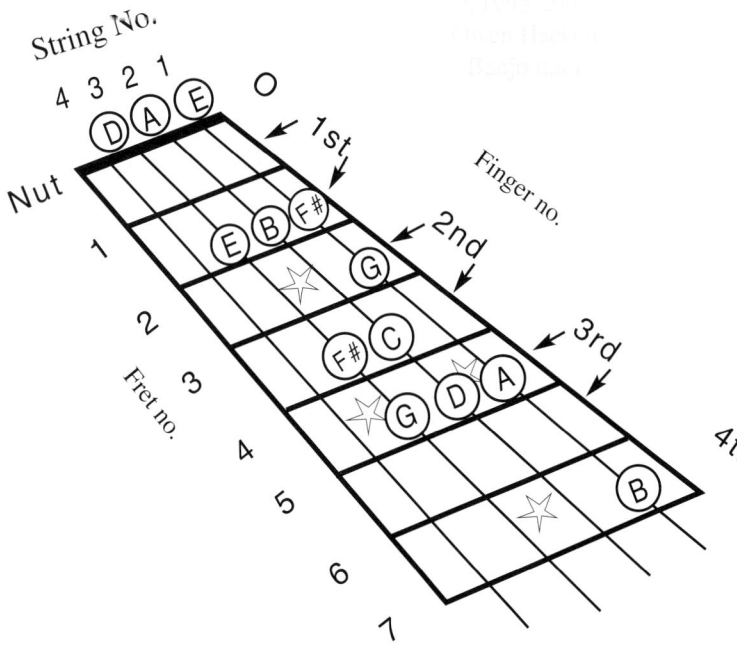

My thanks to John Brady, (flute player) Killeigh, Co Offaly, for this lovely march.
To help you get the timing of the notes correct, try the following:

Crotchets:

2 down & 2 up = ↓↑↓↑ 4 strokes.

Quavers: 1 down & 1 up = ↓↑, 2 strokes.

Dottedquavers:

1 down, 1 up & 1 down = ↓↑↓ 3 strokes.

Semiquavers: 1 stroke, either down or up, depending what it follows, but most of the time it's an up stroke.

Tap your foot twice in each bar, the first beat receiving stronger emphasis, (see guides). Some people might prefer only the one main beat, but to my mind it sounds livelier with the two beats.

EXERCISE 38
PART 2

John Brady's March, in G.

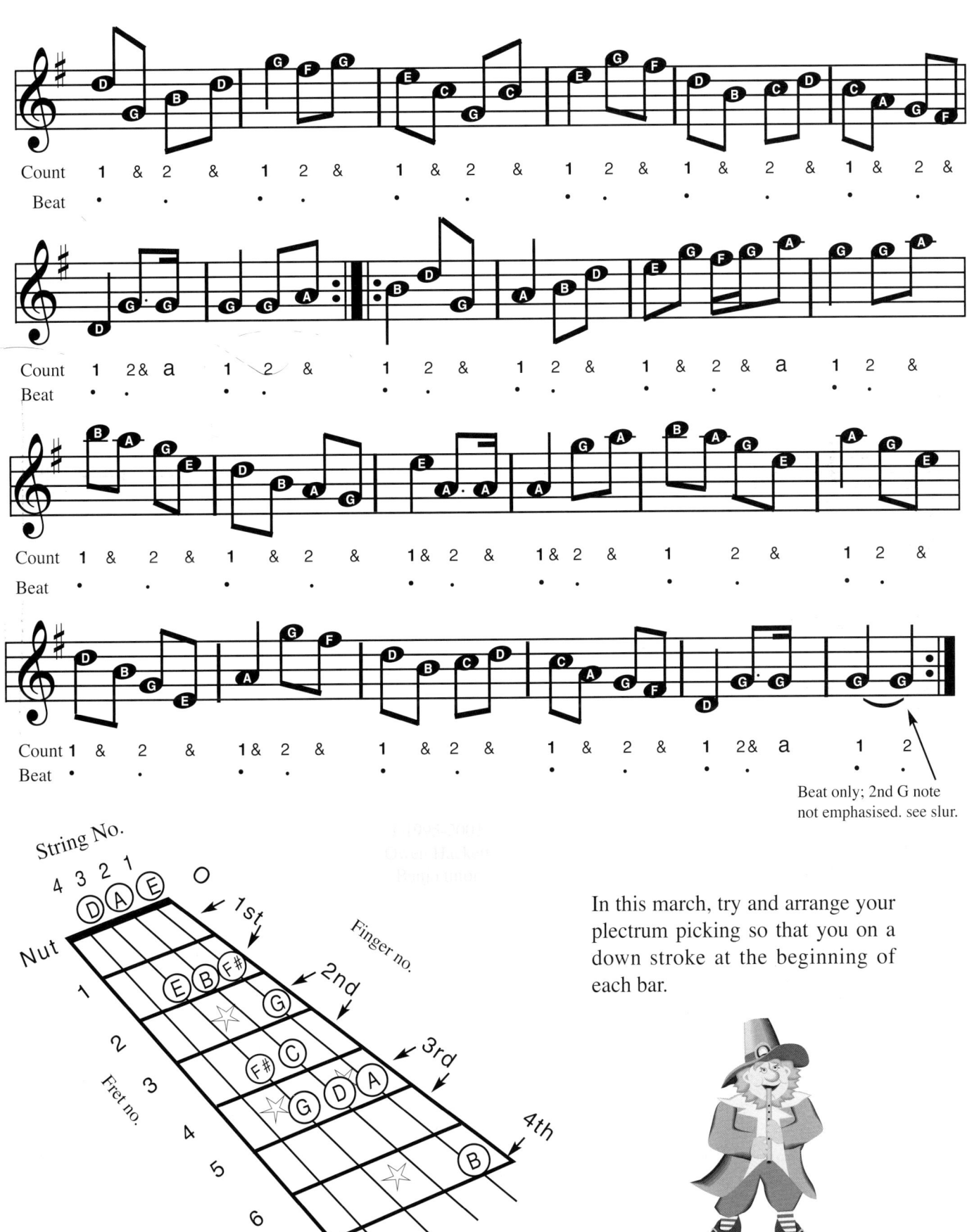

Beat only; 2nd G note not emphasised. see slur.

In this march, try and arrange your plectrum picking so that you on a down stroke at the beginning of each bar.

PLAYING IN DIFFERENT KEYS 1

On this page you will find tips on playing in different keys and playing an octave above normal. The octave playing is useful for band or group work, as it adds variety to the music. Knowing how to play easily in different keys is equally important for accompaniment, in groups etc.

Starting with the 12th fret, position your fingers as shown in the diagram, with your 1st finger on 12th fret acting as the nut, as in the 1st (normal playing) position. Now try and play the **Kerry Polka**, referring back if necessary to the written notes earlier in the tutor.

Now, slide your whole hand back one fret, (1st finger on the 11th fret) and play the tune again, keeping your fingers in the same <u>relative</u> positions. You will obviously be playing the tune one semi-tone lower, in this case C♯ or D♭, the original key being D maj.
One fret lower again, and you play in C maj. and so on.
These keys refer only to tunes originally in D maj. (and using the D finger-shape).

To play a tune that is normally played in G maj. do the very same. First, play it an octave above normal, 12th fret, to get used to using your 1st finger instead of the open strings. Then raise or lower your hand to get different keys relative to G maj. Up 2 frets, you get A maj. down 2 frets gives you F maj. and so on. Some of these keys, (such as C, F & A) can be easily played in the 1st position, others may be a little bit harder to learn and use, especially if you have a long-necked instrument.

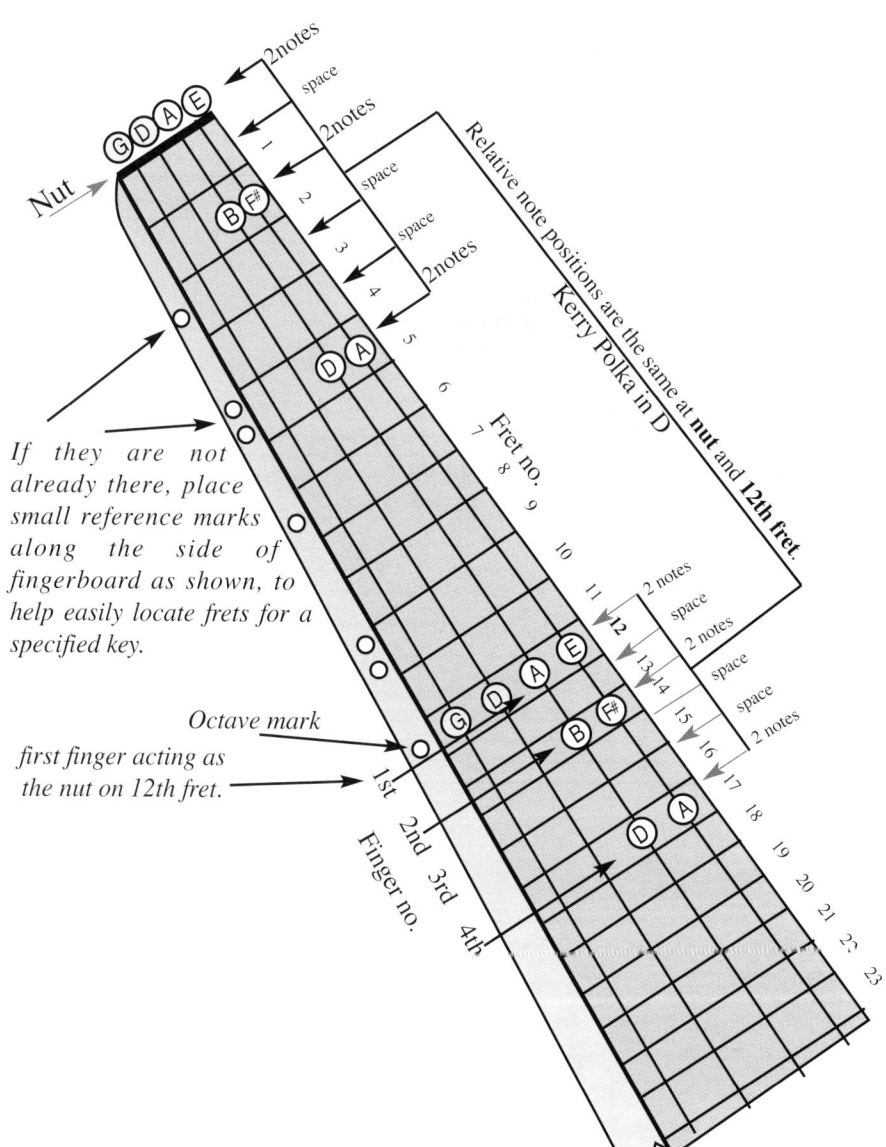

If they are not already there, place small reference marks along the side of fingerboard as shown, to help easily locate frets for a specified key.

Octave mark first finger acting as the nut on 12th fret.

All keys can be played in many other positions around the fretboard using different finger-shape. Finger-shapes are the positions of the notes and where you place your fingers <u>relative to each other</u> to play a tune. An example of this is the relative positions of the notes for the Kerry Polka. See diagram above.

PLAYING IN DIFFERENT KEYS 2

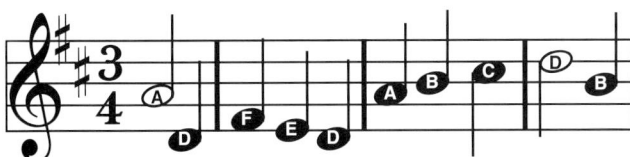

Here are a few notes of Baidin Fheilimi in D to get you started. All the notes for the full tune are shown on the fretboard diagram below.

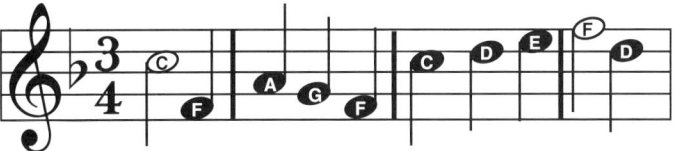

Here it is again in F. All the notes for the full tune are shown on the fretboard diagram below.

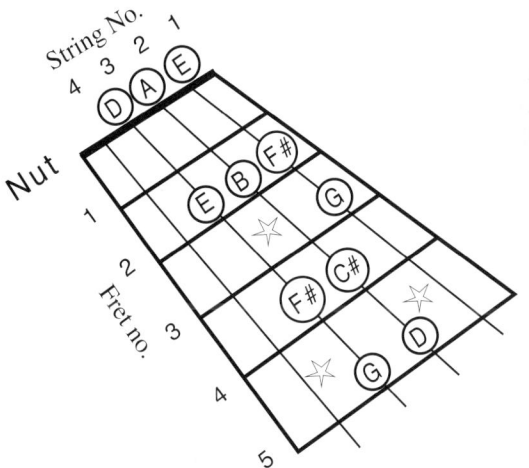

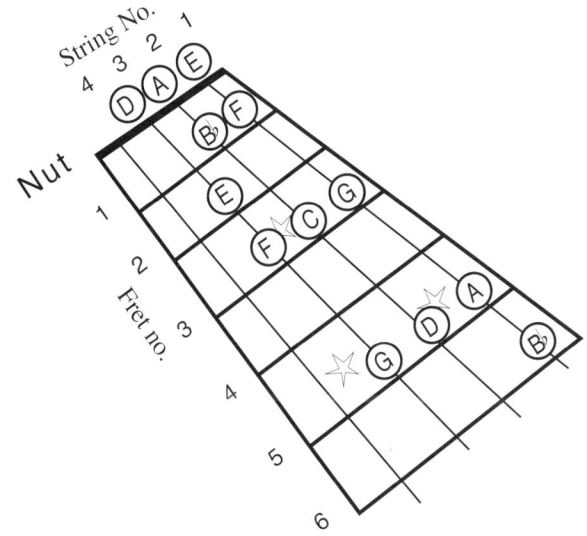

Now try playing the **Dingle Regatta** with 1st finger on the 12th fret (see page 65). There is need to practice sliding the finger into position here, because of the high B. When mastered, play the tune in different positions (keys) for practice.

Baidin Fheilimi is given earlier in the tutor in the key of C.

If you move up one <u>string</u> to 2nd. stay on the 5th fret, and start the tune on the D instead of the G (see relevant lesson), you will be playing in G.

If you move up one string more to 1st, starting on the high A (5 fret) you are playing in D, but there is a problem in that you have to go way up the fingerboard. Instead, start on the open A, 2nd string, play the tune, and you will learn to play in a new position and learn a new finger-shape. See diagrams on accompanying page.

See diagrams also for playing in F maj. Learn these keys off by heart, then apply them to other tunes.

PLAYING IN DIFFERENT KEYS 3

Spancil Hill in B min. (an octave higher)

This 8 with the dotted line above it means play an octave above the written music.

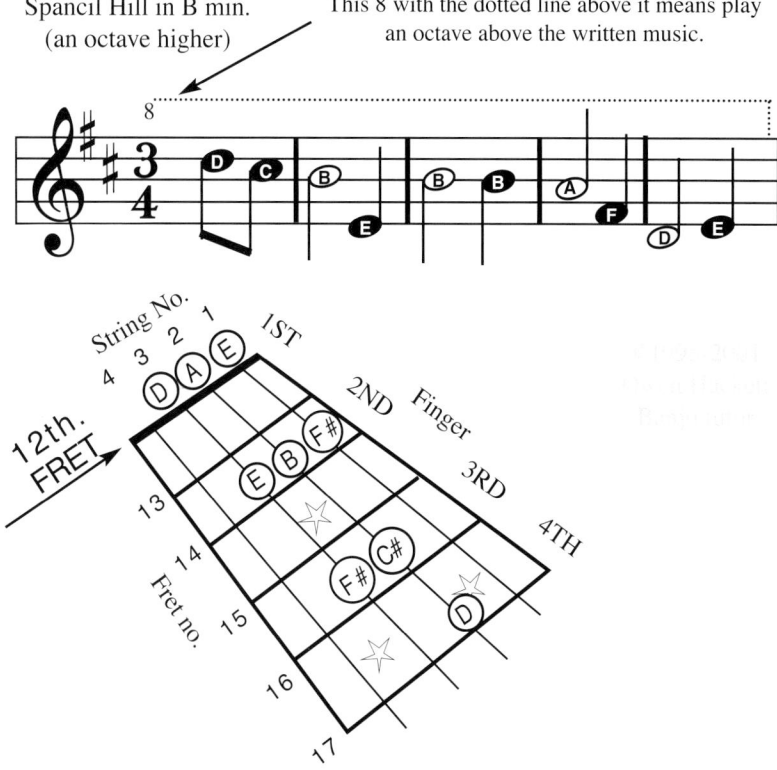

Take your time learning this octave playing. When you have learned the tune, you can practice moving up and down the fingerboard, changing to any key you like using the same finger shapes. Obviously, you can learn different fingershapes at the 1st position but some of these are very hard to master with long necked instruments.

When you feel confident at this level, you can experiment at finding the most suitable place on the fingerboard to play tunes in different keys.

Some people like to use a 'capo'. This is a mechanical device that can be fixed across the strings on the fingerboard, so that the musician can play tunes in different keys, using the same finger-shape and relative note positions as in the 1st normal playing position. For instance, if you play a tune in G normal playing, then fix the capo across the strings at the 2nd fret, the same finger-shape lets you play 2 semi-tones higher in A, and so on. The drawback with this is, if the music or singer you are accompanying, changes key in the medley, the 'capo' has to be re-arranged in order to continue in the new key.

Learning to play without the capo is strongly recommended. It is easier to learn, starting on the octave usually the 12th fret because the frets are closer together and you stay in the same key making it easier for novices to recognise the tune.

Clareen Banjos,
Slieveaun,
Clarinbridge,
Co. Galway,
Ireland.

Tom Cussen

maker

Clareen Banjos

Tel: 00 353 91 796156
Fax: 00 353 91 796931
Inquire for all other instruments

SPECIALLY DESIGNED & MANUFACTURED
FOR THE
TRADITIONAL & FOLK MUSICIAN
STANDARD MODELS AVAILABLE
1 SPECIAL
2 PEARL
3 OYSTER
Tenor banjos Standard and Short Scale
5 String banjos left and right handed.
Colour brochure and price list available
CUSTOMISED MODELS AVAILABLE
TENOR BANJO STRINGS
SPECIALLY DESIGNED FOR IRISH TENOR BANJO TUNING
G.D.A.E.
ALL BANJOS ACCESSORIES AVAILABLE.

CHANGING THE KEY OF A TUNE. (TRANSPOSING.) PART 1

Sometimes a tune might not be suitable for a particular instrument or maybe the player might prefer it in a different key. The following shows how to change the written music, making it easier to learn in the new key. We are using the reel 'The Innocent Child' to work on.

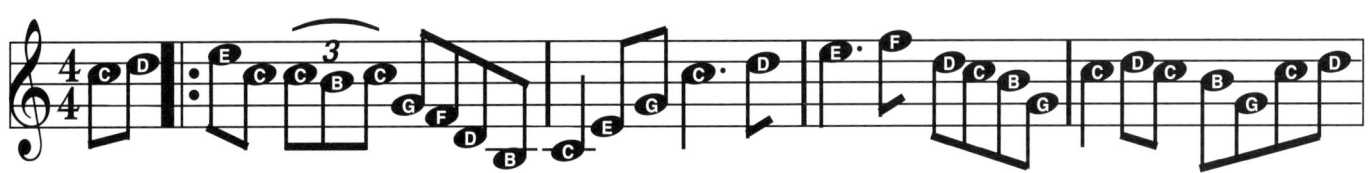

Using a blank music staff, draw in the required key signature signs; key D has two sharps F & C.

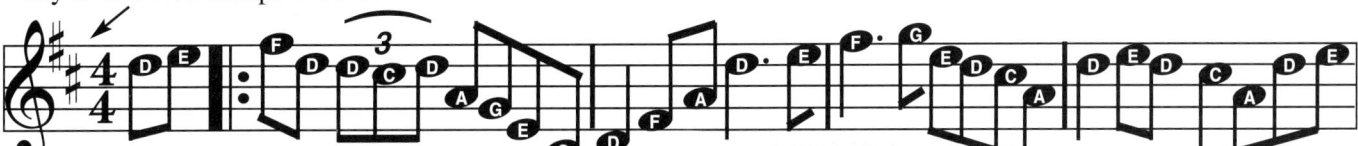

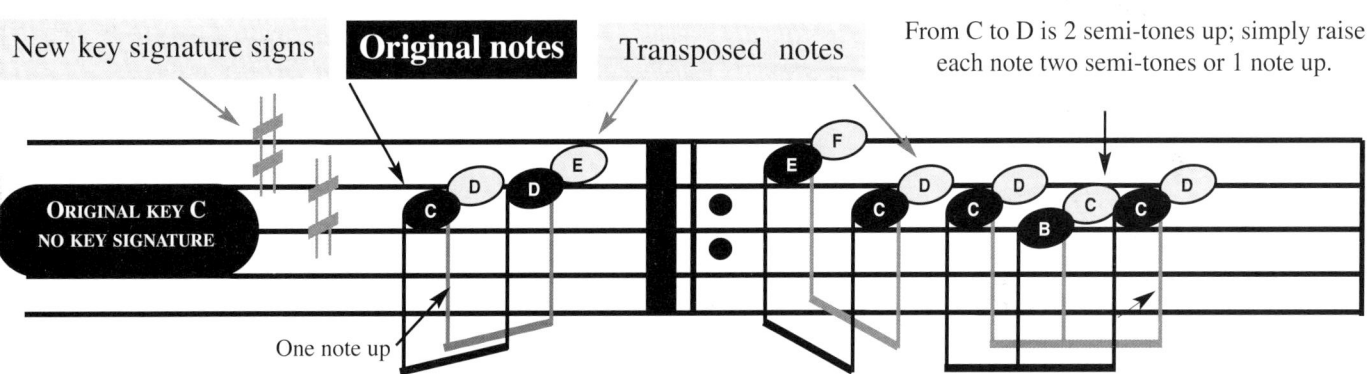

To re-write a given tune in a new key, simply draw a blank staff and put in the <u>key signature</u> of whatever key you want to change to. The example here shows a change from C Maj to D Maj. Count the number of semi-tones from the original to the required key, in this case, <u>two semi-tones</u>. Then re-write the tune in the new blank staff, with all notes two semi-tones higher. ie. from C to C♯= 1 semi-tone; C♯ to D=1 semi-tone, total 2 semi-tones. What to do if only going from C to C♯?=1 semitone: Simply leave all the notes where they are and put in the key signature for C♯= 7 ♯'s.

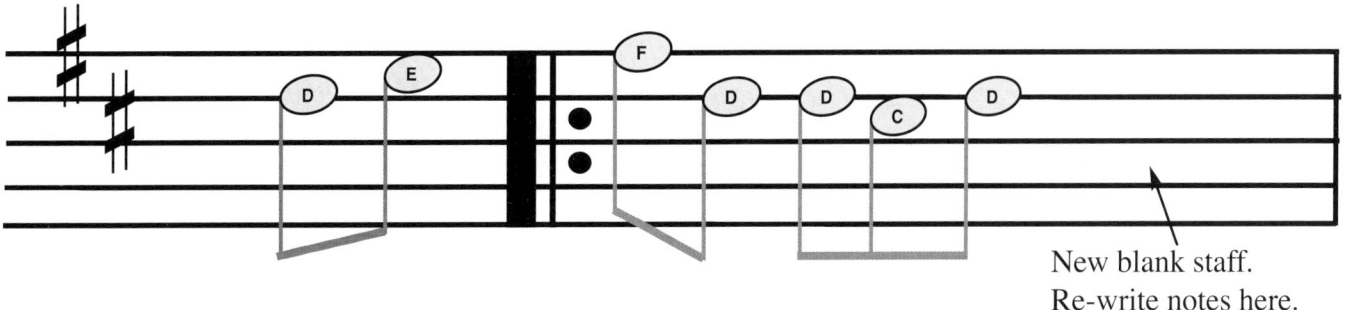

TRANSPOSING
PART 2

Here you see how to change the key of a tune.
Also refer to notes at bottom of previous page.

TRANSPOSING
PART 3

On this page is shown how to transpose notes
with an accidental in them.

MORE BITS AND PIECES

THE VELLUM

Below are instructions on removing an old vellum. The instructions for fitting a new one are on the next page.

If it is a nylon or plastic vellum you are fitting, then it is obvious that **all** the instructions given in the *REPLACING A VELLUM.* page are not relevant. It should go without saying that the instructions referring to the flesh wire and soaking the vellum, allowing it to dry etc, may be ignored. In short, the removing of the old vellum and replacing a new nylon one takes around an hour, (including refitting new strings) then you are ready to play the banjo straight away. That's the advantage of ready-made vellums. The disadvantages are that the tone is not as gentle or soft as the natural skins. Also if your banjo is not a standard size you may find it difficult to get a ready-made vellum to fit it.

Banjo vellums or skins have been know to burst. There is one incident that the author is painfully aware of. Having left his banjo in the warm kitchen he made his way to bed. During the night, he was awakened by a loud bang. It was not until he went to play the banjo the following day, that he realised what had caused the bang. The skin (vellum) had contracted in the heat and burst.

Removing old vellum

1. Remove the resonator
2. Either remove all the tensioning hooks **F** and very carefully place them in the upturned resonator (back) *or* simply loosen them and let them just hang there until you're ready to refit them.
3. Pull the tensioning band **A** up from the body or rim **D**
4. The damaged skin **E** should lift off at this stage
5. Peel the edges of the old skin back and remove the flesh wire **B**

A word of caution

6. Take care not to pull the flesh wire out of shape; these are sometimes not continues unbroken rings, but straight wire curved to shape having the ends loosely joined.

Tip;
If strings are slipping off the bridge or nut, deepen the slots for them, but only very slightly. Take special care with the nut. moisten a cloth with a drop of sewing machine oil and rub on top of nut and bridge to help strings move freely when tuning. ***Protect vellum from oil.***

REPLACING THE VELLUM

Assuming you have removed the strings and bridge, follow this step by step guide on how to remove and replace a vellum
excessive heat can cause vellums to burst

Select a clean skin that's not too thick. Feel it, between thumb and finger. By testing different skins you should be able to tell a good thin one from one that's too thick. This is important if you want the best sound from your instrument.

Fitting new vellum

1. Soak the skin overnight in a basin of clean cold water.
2. Drain surplus water from skin.
3. With banjo resting on a soft surface, place skin evenly over banjo body **D** and tone ring **C** (if there is one on the banjo)
4. Carefully place flesh wire **B** on top of skin and push it down a few mm around the body (rim) **D** of the banjo.
5. Pull the edges of the skin **E** back up around the flesh wire **B** actually enclosing the wire fully.
6. Place the tensioning band **A** over the pulled back edges of the skin. Make sure the edge of skin **E** is *inside* band **A**
7. Alternate between pushing the tensioning band **A** down and pulling the edges of the skin **E** up, until the skin is sitting firmly on the body **D** and /or tone ring **C**
8. Make sure the band **A** is down tight to the enclosed flesh wire **B**
9. Continue pressing band **A** down until it's top is level with surface of vellum sitting on tone ring **C** or body (rim) **D** making sure it is parallel with surface.
10. Be careful not to press band A down too far initially. You must leave room below it for further tensioning of vellum when it has dried. (24 hrs approx)
11. Refit tension hooks **F** and carefully tighten (loosely) each one opposite each other working your way around the (clock) of tension hooks (taking up slack) like so, eg,
    1. O'clock then 7. O'clock;
    5. O'clock then 11. O'clock;
    2. O'c- 8. O'c; 4. O'c- 8. O'c and so on.
12. When this is done, leave to dry before bringing up to the required tension in the same way. don't over tighten or vellum may burst.
13. Fit new strings and tune up. Check tension of vellum after a few days; tighten if required.

Carefully tighten opposite nuts

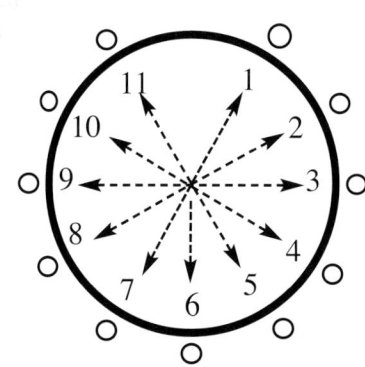

FITTING A VELLUM

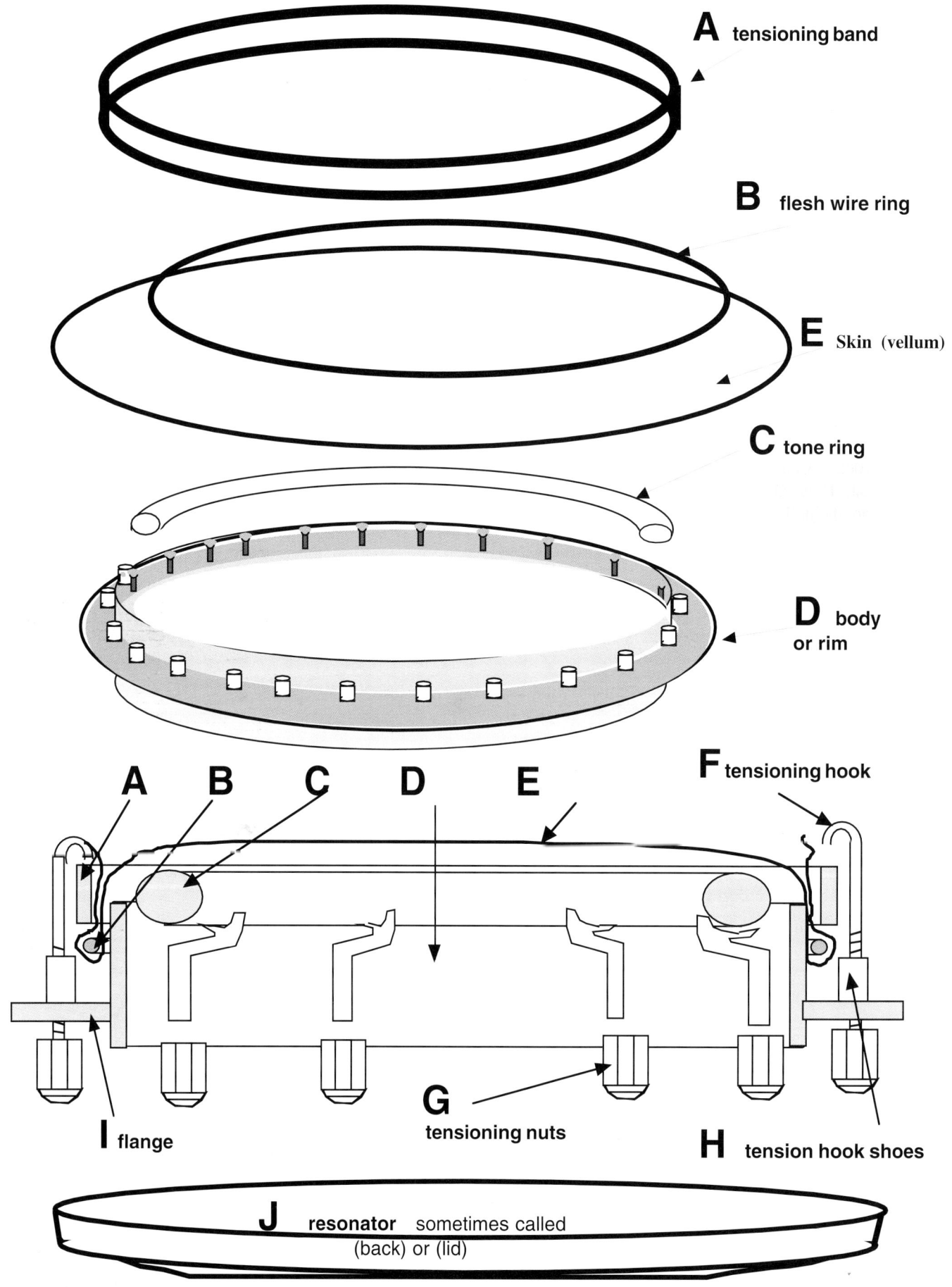

Jigs

89

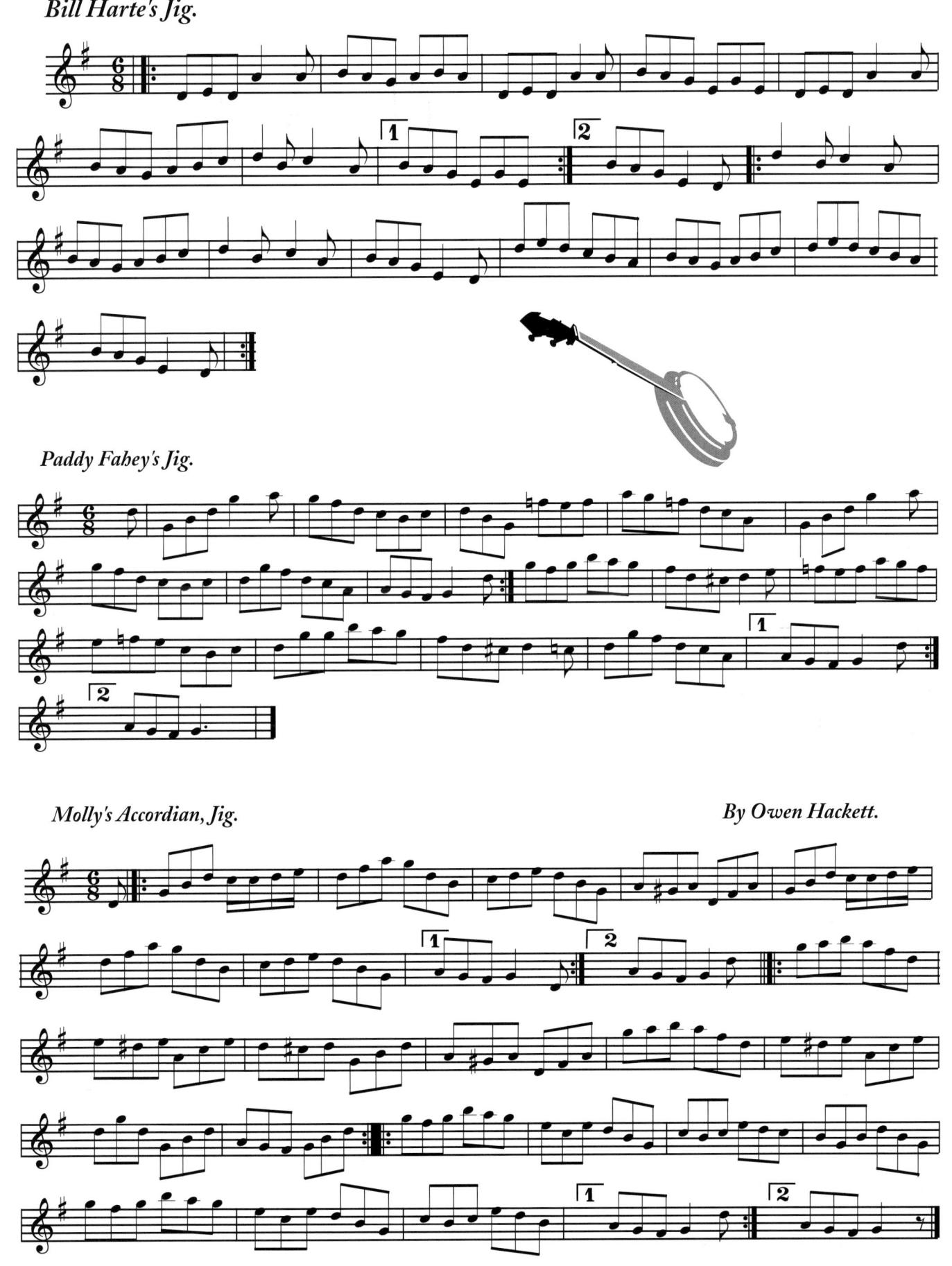

Hornpipes.

The Flowing Tide.

The Athlone Hornpipe.

Sherlock's Hornpipe.

The Good Neighbour.   *By Owen Hackett.*